THE

YARNELL

7

The Seven Core Decisions for
Extraordinary Living

Amy Yarnell Carter

Illustrations by Dylan Russell
Graphics by Drew Haley

ISBN: 978-0-9991165-1-7
ISBN: 978-0-9991165-0-0 (ebook)

Praise for *The Yarnell 7*

5-Star Reviews

What an incredible treat this read was for me. I couldn't put it down. Working with Mark personally, this book brought back the fondest memories for me. And, a few belly laughs as well. Such wisdom that Amy captured as she experienced life with Mark Yarnell. I lived vicariously through her stories often transporting me to that place of love and laughter. The content was well placed throughout the book and when I finished, I felt so complete. A book I will read again and again. If you are doing life, this book is a must for your library!

—Mary Beth Gasser

Extraordinary read by Amy Yarnell Carter that I highly recommend! Greatness surely runs in the Yarnell DNA. After having the privilege and honor of working closely with Mark Yarnell the last 14 months of his life, I feel Amy literally bottled up and channeled his recipe for living your best life. Well written with practical tools, compassion, and the healing Yarnell humor. Don't walk, but run to devour this life transforming read.

—Tina Perrman

YES! Amy Yarnell Carter knocked it out of the ballpark with TY7! It is an awesome book, a must-read for everyone from 9 to 90 years young! A very well-written, thought out book with the perfect amount of anecdotes sprinkled among the gems of knowledge. This is a book you won't put down!

—Cary G. Waggoner, CPA and Staci D. Waggoner, CPA

Amy Yarnell Carter has written a guidebook for those of us looking to be successful AND happy in our lives. Her understanding and experience of tremendous loss and personal growth is an inspiration to those of us looking for that same outlook. We often struggle focusing on what we don't have and compare that to what we truly want. Ms.

Yarnell teaches us that we can really have what we want; we just have to change the way we think. This absolute realization that we are in charge of our lives and our decisions is powerful stuff and when you sit and think about it, we all realize it's so TRUE. Our lives. Our responsibility. Brilliant!!!

—RK

Finally a book that encourages us to take responsibility for our lives, take action, and live it to the fullest. Reading this book gave me so many insights into my life especially the parts I was avoiding and keeping small. It is a fast read, well written, and a useful resource. Easy to go back and pull up reminders. Excellent quotations that really hit home.

—Heather Bierly

I wish I had read this 2 decades ago. I wouldn't have wasted so much time in unproductive directions and decisions, and I certainly would have smiled more. I had the opportunity to hear Mark Yarnell speak, and I remember him being very engaging. And that's in front of a bunch of 18 year olds that wanted nothing more than to get their diploma and be done with high school. I highly recommend picking this up and reading it. Get several so you can have one at work, one at home, one for traveling, and refer back to it often. Calling this book simply "self help" is like saying toilet paper is useful.

—David D.

The Yarnell 7 is a great tribute to Amy's father, Mark Yarnell, but additionally TY7 is an excellent guide for simple, realistic strategies for upgrading your ordinary life to a more conscious, decision focused, "extraordinary" life. Amy gives 7 practical, yet powerful, decisions, or choices, to live life at the highest level. TY7 is an easy read filled with sound decision models. Amy is motivating and filled with enthusiasm in her writing. I would definitely recommend this book to others.

—Lisa Cragar, MS, LPC

I don't usually read books but this book has already changed my perception on life. This book is going to be a life saver to so many people that are struggling with perceptions in life and just simply needed someone to spell it out so that it is relatable and easier to make a change for the better. I already have a list of people that will benefit greatly from the information within TY7! Thank you so much for helping me see ME!

—Alexis

This book is amazing. Amy has taken 7 simple steps to living an incredible life and made them easy to follow. If you want to change your life, follow The Yarnell 7. Keep it close at hand so you can pick it up at any moment. Guaranteed to change your life. There are worksheets to walk you through the Yarnell 7 Decision Maker. The writing is direct and honest. I really enjoyed the anecdotes. A must read!

—Amazon Customer

At every moment of every day, we have a choice about the decisions we make. It's the combination of these choices small and large that comprise the totality of our life. In her book, The Yarnell 7, Amy Yarnell beautifully honors the life lessons taught by her father that informed her view of the world. She outlines a clear and achievable process for achieving the life you want through inspiring stories and actionable worksheets. Definitely worth the read!

—S. Peppercorn

Wonderful! An enthusiastic guide to take charge of your life and make it "extraordinary". Very inspirational with personal experiences and motivating quotes. Decisions explained simple but perfectly and personable. Love!

—Virginia Gray

This book is life changing! I truly enjoyed reading it. It is beautifully and simplistically written. At the same time, the message is powerful. Live life to the fullest. Everyday! I recommend this book to everyone.

—Julie D.

This is the life advice we all need. Carter gets right to the heart of how we can all improve our lives and positively effect the lives of the people around us.

—Joy

This book is genius. It puts a positive spin on everything in life. Completely life changing. Recommend this book to everyone!

—Kira Fell

Way to go Amy Yarnell Carter! The Yarnell 7 is a beautiful tribute to your Dad's extraordinary life and the continuation of his legacy!

—Christine P.

To Dad

TABLE OF CONTENTS

Dear Reader,

Thank you for purchasing *The Yarnell 7*. I am thrilled that you have made the decision to live an extraordinary life!

In order to ensure your success, I have incorporated multiple worksheets within the text and included them at the end of this book as well. Also, please keep in mind that there is a "Notes" section in the back and I encourage you to write down any ideas or questions in that section. If you run out of room on your worksheets or you are reading the ebook version, please go to "Worksheets" at www.TheYarnell7.com and download some more for free!

In addition, if you would like to stay up to date with *The Yarnell 7* and all things extraordinary, please enter your email address at www.TheYarnell7.com and I will be happy to send you all of the updates.

I am celebrating this first release with raffles and drawings that I would love for you to be a part of as well. There is a link at the back of the book with more information so make sure to check that out when you are finished reading *The Yarnell 7*.

Congratulations on making this first turning-point decision and I look forward to learning all about your successes!

INTRODUCTION:

The POWER of DECISIONS

The day my father passed away, I sat in his office, reeling with the shock and grief of my loss, and as I chose songs off his iPad for his funeral and thought about his amazing life, three simple words ran through my head:

He did it.

I quickly stood up from the couch in his office downstairs, walked to the window, and gazed out at the beautiful Okanagan Lake below. As I looked at the beauty that surrounded my father every day of his life, I thought again, *He really did pull the whole thing off. He did it!* And though tears were falling down my face, I smiled.

Many of you knew Mark Yarnell from his books or saw him speak; you knew him personally or you worked with him professionally; but no matter how you knew him, you knew he was an extraordinary person.

For those of you who didn't know him, Mark Yarnell was a DYNAMO. He was a paraglide pilot, a best-selling author, an amazing public speaker, a powerhouse network marketer and noted philanthropist. He was fearless and wild but also loving and kind. He was off-the-charts brilliant and his laugh was contagious. Everyone who knew him wanted to be around the man as often as possible—he was so enthusiastic and interesting and fun that you couldn't help having a wonderful day if you spent it with him.

Although he was extremely successful and extraordinary and I looked up to him a great deal, I also wondered many, many times over the course of my forty-one years if his outlook on life would ever change. In some ways, I watched him like a child watches a science experiment; his passion was so powerful and his excitement so palpable that I watched him and wondered if he would ever lose even one small bit of his astounding energy as his life proceeded on such an extraordinary course of bliss. I certainly hoped he wouldn't, because he was so incredibly happy, fun and full of life, but I also wondered if it was really, truly possible to live in that state of perpetual excitement … forever.

And the day I realized that "he did it" and that the outcome of all he had lived was not merely monetary success but true life success, I knew I had a job to do. Over the next two years, I reflected on what made him so incredibly different from everyone else because I knew that if I could distill his WHY's and HOW's for extraordinary living, that I would owe it to humanity to write this book. As a result, it is my hope that every single person has a chance and a choice to model the way he chose to live his life and therefore, a chance to lead extraordinary lives themselves.

From a very young age, my dad programmed me on purpose, to *have* a purpose. And because I was young and looked at my father like he was a god (if not God Himself), I believed what he told me. I fell for his ideas about life, hook, line and sinker—and thank God! I had the great advantage to have learned all of *The Yarnell 7* in my formative years and that is why it is so very important to me to ensure that you and your children have the same opportunities I have enjoyed.

This book is your ticket to live an extraordinary life. There is simply no reason for you to live any less of a life than the very best—and now. Take a deep breath, because it all starts with you making a very simple decision. You must decide right now if you want to live an extraordinary life. Let me be clear: this is your *choice*. You either decide that you will move forward with how you are living right now … OR you decide that you can do, be, and have everything that you desire.

The decisions that you make every single day and every single moment are the decisions that produce the framework for your entire life. Events and people outside of your control may seem to dictate your days and moments and even years, but ultimately it is *your* decisions that create the foundation for who you are and the reality of your own life.

At this moment, I am convinced that the following decision is the single most important one that you will ever make:

You decide that your life is already so fantastic you can't imagine making any improvements, and so you set this book back down (or click out of the page, whichever the case may be);

OR

You decide right now that you will read *The Yarnell 7*, move to extraordinary heights and live the best life possible.

So let me be completely clear: If you want to live an extraordinary life, read on. If you know your life could be awesome and you are ready to make the ultimate decisions that will enable you to reach that state of awesomeness, you are in the right place, right here and right now. **Read on**. If you want to continue down the path of uncertainty and haphazard happiness—or, as I like to call it, the "teeter-totter of happiness"—put it down. X out. Your **decision.**

But remember: every choice you make has an impact on those around you and so when you make the decision to read this book, your life—and everyone else's life around you—will change forever!

So what will it be?

If you just chose to move forward with reading this book and change your life (and the world) forever, CONGRATULATIONS!

The first thing you need to understand is the subtitle of this book. Please note that it is not called *The Seven Principles/Values/Mindsets/Habits for Extraordinary Living*, but rather *The Seven Core **Decisions** for Extraordinary Living*.

That's because this life of yours is exactly that: YOURS. And it is the act of making decisions about you and your life that changes everything!

There is a certain freedom that comes along with the understanding that everything you do or think is in fact a decision on your part. Isn't there?

Let's get started!

DECISION #1

YES!

"You create your own reality."
—Mark Yarnell

One summer when I was a teenager, Dad bounded in my room (as usual) and exclaimed loudly, "GOOD MORNING, HONEY! IT'S GONNA BE A GREAT DAY!" And I, in typical teenage fashion, rolled over and pulled the covers over my head. He sat down beside me and said, "Here's the deal … every day when you wake up, you have a decision to make. You either decide it is going to be a great day, or you decide it is going to be a bad day. Your decision." With that, he bounced out of the room.

So I decided it would indeed be a great day. From that time forward, when there was a morning that I did not make that decision, I was acutely aware of my own responsibility. And life shifted.

If you truly want to live an **extraordinary** life, you must greet your whole world with one word, and that is: "YES!" And this is why: the world around you is made up of what you make it. That's right—you are the person giving your entire life meaning!

Mark Yarnell always said he lived a "Zip-a-Dee-Doo-Da" life and that he woke up every morning and said "YES!" and then he continued on with his day with a whole series of YES's.

"YES! It's gonna be a great day!" "Yes! I'm going to go get chipotle sauce and fries!" "YES! I'm going to do a series of three-way calls!" and "YES! I am going to go run off that mountain and fly with the eagles!"

DECISION BY DEFINITION

Your life is made up of a series of perceptions that you **decide** to make. This is the single largest freedom that you can ever realize and actualize. When you change your perceptions, you will shift your own reality. If you get this, your life will dramatically change—and YES! I mean dramatically!

The normal sense of responsibility, the one we are all accustomed to, is that we are responsible for our actions. Clearly, we all know that we decide to go brush our teeth, we decide to go to work, and we decide to eat dinner after work. All day long we make decisions that guide our lives in a most basic way.

However, the difference between an ordinary life and an extraordinary life is realizing that we are making decisions through the definitions we give our surroundings. We are deciding how we view our life by defining the world around us. This life is 100 percent about our perceptions first and our actions second. (But don't worry—actions will be discussed in the next chapter!)

That is one step deeper than just being responsible for our actions, isn't it? Now, take a moment and let it sink in: how you perceive or define your life, and every moment within it, is your **decision**. Now, given that reality, it is easy to understand that your entire life is your responsibility. (And don't worry—we'll discuss more about responsibility in chapter three!)

You can either wake up and declare "IT IS GOING TO BE A GREAT DAY!" or you can wake up and stumble around, bemoaning the fact that you are awake and it is just another day. Your choice.

When I was a little girl, about three years old, I was out in the driveway, "driving" my little bike and going the "speed lemon" (three-year-old speak for "speed limit") and somehow managed to tip over. I looked down and discovered a good-sized scratch on my knee, oozing, of all things, blood! I ran to the porch where my parents were sitting, crying and scared. I remember distinctly that my dad bent over and wiped the blood from my knee. Then he held it out in front of my face, smiled and said:

"It's just blood."

My very first lesson in perception was this: When you fall down, stand up from your momentary reaction to gravity, note that blood is just that—blood—and then slap a Band-Aid on that scratch and go ride the "speed lemon" again; simply bandage your knee up and head out!

You see, your perceptions and definitions are everything in life because how you act, the decisions you make and how you react to uncontrolled forces dictate your experience. Because you control your own perceptions, your reality becomes your own.

Let's take another simple example so this can sink in:

There is a chair. The chair is a small, antique, light pink chair and it is sitting in your living room. It is just a chair. It has no intrinsic value in and of itself other than you can sit on it to enjoy a nice cup of tea.

Okay, now check this out:

This very same small, antique, light pink chair is sitting in your living room. This chair was given to you as a gift for your thirtieth birthday from your now-deceased grandmother who raised you as her very own.

Now let's look at the chair: it is still just a chair, and its only true value is one which you have placed on it. But *now* the chair has a completely different definition. I look at the chair, it's a chair; you look at the chair, it's your grandmother. **This is how all of life is: the only value in things and people and everything in your environment is labeled by you**.

Okay, now look around and realize that your reality is your own reality—not mine, not your Aunt Tilly's and not your boss's. Yours.

Are you starting to see your responsibility now? Once you realize that your life is your responsibility, and that you **create** it, you must make the decision to embrace that fact.

Here is how you do it: Every time you have a negative thought and every time you start to complain, you STOP and turn it around.

Let's take another example:

You wake up and groan. Realizing that you create your own reality and that "YES!" is your default exclamation for life, you quickly change your attitude and you say, "YES! This is going to be a great day!" You get up, whistle while you get ready for the day, jump in the car, crank the tunes and happily head to work.

While you are having a dance-off with yourself in the car, something outside of your control happens! UH OH! Another driver pulls out in front of you and this simple act impedes your happy progress. Immediately, your hackles are up. You might even cuss or yell. You follow the slow driver all the way to your most frequented coffee shop, seething in anger the whole way … and by now, your happy "YES" has turned into an absolute "NO."

You park, get out of the car, slam your car door and walk in. You order your coffee and because you are still completely annoyed by the inept driver, you grunt at the person behind the front desk and grumble "thank you" as you collect your change. You get to work and continue to grumble all the way down the hall to your desk.

Now let's say you haven't yet read *The Yarnell 7* (which, so far, you haven't—not all the way, anyway) and let's take a look at the absurdity of this whole situation.

Without understanding and **deciding** that you create your own reality, you are essentially making the following declaration about your morning: "It was a great morning and I whistled all the way to my car and then some #%$@% pulled out in front of me and now my day sucks."

Are you kidding me? You were happy and now your day is awful because another person pulled out in front of you on the road?

But this type of reaction to other people and events happens time and time again! Not just in the car but everywhere! It can be a driver of another vehicle, a text you receive that uses periods instead of exclamations and smiley faces, a crappy email from your client or coworker. And this, the STUFF of LIFE, is what you allow to put you on the down side of the "teeter-totter of happiness"!

We are UP and then we are DOWN. We respond and we react to life as if we have no choice in the matter ... which is ridiculous when it comes down to it.

Now, this is how it goes when you realize and decide that you create your own reality:

You wake up and declare "YES! This is going to be a great day!" You make coffee, whistle in the bathroom while you get ready for work, hop in your car and go. Then the guy who doesn't care about the fact that you actually have to get somewhere, pulls out in front of you and you feel your habituated response immediately!! You are MAD. This guy doesn't care that you are on a timeline—what a jerk!

Now, Decision Makers of *The Yarnell 7* will do one of two things to resolve the whole internal problem (which appears to be external to everyone else).

1. You either shrug your shoulders, accept the fact that the other driver is not in your control, that getting angry is not going to change anything about this situation, and embrace the awesome experience of listening to more great tunes on the way to work;

OR

2. You **remove** yourself from the situation by pulling over and hanging out for a bit on the side of the road.

Let me say this again: in every situation in your life that you deem emotionally upsetting or dispiriting or any other yucky feeling that you have that is seemingly out of your control, you have two choices:

1. You can either decide to change your perception of the situation

OR

2. You extricate yourself from the situation.

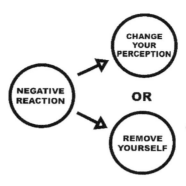

Now, let's go back to the "jerk" who pulled out in front of you.

Let's say you are apt to get angry when people pull out in front of you or drive slowly in front of you and so your immediate, uncontrolled reaction is extreme anger and because you are a human being who places a whole lot of value in how other people drive, your habitual perception of "you jerk" is not something you can change immediately. Fine then, remove yourself through simple tools.

My dad was very "spirited" while driving his car and other drivers did make him just a tad bit hyper and so, knowing that he created his own reality by perception, and because dealing with other people on the road was not his emotional strong suit, he developed two tools to extricate himself from the situation, one proactive tool and one reactive tool.

First, he always proactively left the house early to be somewhere. This way he wouldn't have any pressure on the road from running late. Second, when a driver pulled out in front of him or he was stuck behind someone who was driving a speed that he deemed was too slow, do you know what he did? He pulled over.

That simple: he pulled over. Because he wasn't running late and he loved music, he had the time to just pull over and wait for the driver to get ahead of him so that he could maintain his space (and speed) and therefore, his immediate happiness!

When you are stuck in a situation that is seemingly out of your control and causes distress, you let go of it either through your *perception* or by *removing* yourself from the situation.

Now let's say that Dad couldn't pull over because there was no place to pull over and the driver in front of him was slowing him down enough that he was no longer early to his self-appointed breakfast meeting. Now, this particular habitual response was very hard for him to control which is why he had proactive and reactive tools. (We all know how this feels … we have a negative reaction and we do not feel able to stop it.) Your habitual negative reaction seems to be a crazy-making monster that has taken control of your state of mind, and you can't seem to change your perception, and you literally can't remove yourself! Then what?

This is what Dad would do when he couldn't change his perception and he couldn't remove himself from the situation: he would make the **decision** to…

Let it go.

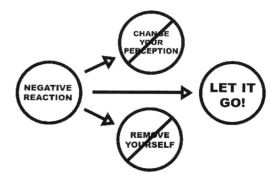

You *let it go and move on down the road*! Drop it; it's over. If you fall victim to your own habitual response, do not hold on to it. Do not provoke it by thinking about it. Do not ruin one more moment of your precious life on a nonsensical habitual response. Do not, I repeat, do not play it like a broken record or rewind it like a movie in your head right now or ever. This is not a movie or a record, this is your life.

> *"Remember happiness doesn't depend upon who you are or what you have; it depends solely on what you think."*
> —Dale Carnegie

So in the case of the rotten driver, you realize that your life is actually just that: your own life. And therefore, you refuse to let this annoyance affect any other part of your day. (After all, you just made the decision to let it impact you for twenty minutes!) When you arrive at the coffee store, you decide again that this is, in fact, a great day (just as it was twenty minutes ago at your house before the inept driver entered your path) and you bound into the store, and get your coffee. While the employee of the store is making your change, you say, "Is this the best day

EVER, or what?" Then you give a big smile and a wink and bound out the door to your car and continue on your way.

Now, you have not only set up yourself for a great day, but you have also set up the employee at the coffee shop to have a great day too! How's that for excellent? (More on this incredible contagion later!)

So let's break things down again.

1. There is an experience, thing, or thought that seemingly causes you upset, irritation, anger, stress or anything else on the not-so-positive spectrum of human emotions.
2. Recognize that you have just placed your own value on the experience, thing, or thought, because your reality is your own reality and no one else has the power to create it or change it.
3. Either
   a. Change your perception (take the value away and give it another definition)
   b. Extricate yourself from the situation, thing or thought, by literal removal from the circumstance
   c. And in the case you can't do either one, LET IT GO!

You can apply these tools from the simplest and most benign circumstances (like while you are having a temper tantrum in your car), and you can also apply them to very important parts of your life like your family and friends.

I have a friend who is constantly being bombarded by her family's self-created dramas and it makes her crazy! When we discuss the latest drama, I remind her that she has two options and she totally gets it. She takes the situation at hand and either changes her perception to "My family members sure are all about the drama but I don't have to be" OR she removes herself from the drama, depending on what the current situation is. She decides to create her own reality on a daily basis.

It doesn't matter if it is a road-rage-issue or a family-drama-issue or a boss-is-crazy issue or a teenage-kid-issue. You still make the ultimate decision to say "YES! I create my own reality! I will now either change the way I am looking at this situation or I will remove myself from it. And in the cases where I can't seem to do either one, I will move on down the road!"

Read this carefully:

Man is made and unmade by himself. In the armory of thought he forges the weapons which will destroy him. He also creates the tools with which he will build for himself heavenly mansions of joy and strength and peace. By the right choice and true application of thought, man ascends to the Divine Perfection; by the abuse and wrong application of thought, he descends below the level of the beast. Between these two extremes are all the grades of character, and man is their maker and their master.

—James Allen

As a Man Thinketh

One More Big Tip:

Sometimes it is very difficult to extricate yourself from a situation (you can't pull over) and sometimes it is also very difficult to change a feeling because it is a habitual response. This process will become easier as you become a Decision Maker of *The Yarnell 7*, but that takes practice! And then, sometimes you will still run into situations where you'll even have a hard time letting it go.

If you feel you can't change your perception or extricate yourself from the situation and you feel that you are holding on to it rather than dropping it from your psyche, here is what you do:

CHANGE YOUR FOCUS.

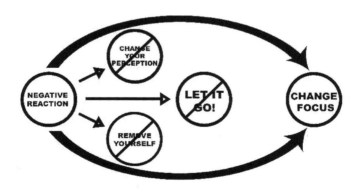

There are two situations in life that are extremely difficult to deal with and if you are going through them, you will be inclined to say "Yes I get it, but ..." to everything you just read. Given these two situations, that reaction of dismissal is completely understandable and it would be remiss of me to ignore them. They are:

ILLNESS AND GRIEF

On Illness

My dad admitted years before he passed away that he didn't feel very good. Now, from a man who does not speak of anything on the lower end of a teeter-totter, this was a very shocking moment for me. He was visibly irritated with the whole thing. He never had a doctor and he did not believe in living "in the system" which for him, was defined by being diagnosed and treated with prescription medications. He was not on any prescriptions and he did not go to doctors unless minor things occurred like say, having a paragliding accident!

After a heated discussion (the whole illness thing was not a happy topic for my dad), I convinced him that seeing a doctor might help with his quality of life. And so, he went and he discovered that he was, in fact, ill.

Now he had a whole new experience and one that would seem to most people, to be out of his control. So how did he create his own reality in the midst of illness?

By doing two things:

1. Researching only that which would make him well and
2. By changing his **focus** from his illness to his wellness and continuing to live happily.

One day in my late twenties, I realized that my heart rate sure did seem to be high (and had for quite some time), and that my head really did seem to be shaking, and WOW it was also kind of weird that my tongue was shaking too! Upon these realizations, I thought to myself: "Self, you might need to go visit a doctor." And so I did.

The nurse took my heart rate and vitals and such and left the room. As I was waiting for the doctor to come in my room to discuss the situation, I heard someone out in the hall say "EKG!" I thought to myself, "Uh oh, someone out there isn't doing so hot!" And then the next thing I knew, my doctor and nurse were in my room, placing some kind of metal and paper things on my chest and hooking me up to some crazy looking contraption! I was mystified. Turns out, my resting heart rate had been 138 and after the blood tests came back, I was diagnosed with Graves disease and sent to an endocrinologist.

Being my dad's child, here is what I did: after I was given the options on how to treat the disease (either surgical removal of my thyroid or Radioactive Iodine treatment), I researched only how to get well, I changed my focus and continued to live happily.

In the case of my dad and myself, we followed the same path: move on and move up. You see, in the case of illness, we still have two options: either change our perceptions or extricate ourselves from the problem. I can hear you now, "I am sick, Amy, I can't extricate myself from the illness and not only that, I feel like crap!" You are correct in your belief of your current reality (as always) but, you must move on.

If you are ill, I have some advice: do not become your illness. Do not define yourself by it, do not walk around or lay around thinking about it. Do two things: do everything you can to make yourself well and do everything you can to change your focus and to live happily.

In today's technological world, we are so fortunate to have an incredible amount of research and knowledge at our fingertips. Google is an awesome tool for us but only if we use it to our advantage. Dad and I could have easily googled all about how bad our illnesses were and all about how bad our treatments would be, but we chose not to do that.

What you focus on is what you experience. For example, when you are ill and you only have two options for treatment, you need to choose one of those options. Do the research on the pros and cons if you must, and discuss the pros and cons with your health care professional and then make a decision. But do not get stuck in the muck of the ill people online. If you are ill, you have two choices: you can either solve it, and focus on wellness and all of the awesome things in your life, OR you can lay down and define yourself an ill person.

Remember: you create your own reality and you may not think that you have chosen to be ill and that may be a total logjam situation, but, but, but … how you deal with the illness is your **decision** and that does become your reality. You must change your focus and continue to live happily as much as you possibly can!

"Whatever condition we are in, we must
always do what we want to do, and if we want to go
on a journey, then we must do so and not worry about our
condition, even if it's the worst possible condition, because, if
it is, we're finished anyway, whether we go on the journey or not,

and it's better to die having made the journey we've been
longing for than to be stifled by our longing."
—Thomas Bernhard, Concrete

In the case of Dad: He was ill, he knew it, he did everything he could to increase the quality of his life and he kept living happily. His focus was not on his illness (unless it was on his wellness). In fact, his death was a complete and TOTAL shock to me and everyone else. I, like so many other people, had spoken to him within the twenty-four hours before he was in the hospital and everything seemed absolutely normal. Of course, normal for him, was bouncing off the walls, excitedly talking about his next project and sending me links and all sorts of things. So when I got the call that he was in the hospital and things might not go so well, I was on a plane within hours in complete and utter disbelief.

There is something you need to know about the last hours of his life, not because I want you to be sad or to feel my sadness, but because it was truly a testament to the power of creating your own reality.

I arrived at the hospital at 10 p.m. on March 2, 2015. He was awake and ready for me, and was in his usual excited state even lying on the hospital bed with tubes in his nose (which I know made him absolutely crazy). As tears were falling out of my eyes, I noticed he was kind of hyper … I assumed he was trying to stay UP for me, and I knew it was because he did not want me to feel what I was feeling.

He didn't want me to feel pain, and so he was acting completely normal and bouncy in his hospital bed. I simply said, "Dad, don't let me get you all excited."

He cocked his head to the side and asked, "What do you mean, honey?"

And nervously I replied, "Well just don't let me get you all amped up!"

He actually CHUCKLED and said, "Oh honey, don't be silly, **you** can't do that, <u>only **I** can do that</u>."

He had become so habituated to taking total responsibility for his perceptions and his state of being and living, that on his literal deathbed, he reminded me of this truth and lived it.

At 10:02 a.m. the next morning, he was gone.

And with that, let's talk about what is the most difficult emotion that I believe we can ever face as human beings:

On Grief

Over the last two years, I have noticed that grief doesn't make much of an appearance into any of the positive thinking and being books (and I have read a lot of them). I think that's because grief is usually taken as a topic by itself and not something to touch on lightly. But given that I am writing *The Yarnell 7* and because I am my father's daughter, I have some tools in my arsenal that I would like to share.

Grief is an experience we all have to deal with eventually. When someone dies, clearly we cannot change it, nor can we extricate ourselves from it and oftentimes it doesn't feel like we can let it go either. This is the ULTIMATE LOGJAM. So given that we can't take it away, and Psychology 101 tells us that we can't completely ignore it either, we have to learn the best way to live with it ... and that's just it: **we live**. And maybe we aren't able to live happily quite as easily for awhile, but what we are able to do is control the amount of time we focus on it.

Now don't hear me wrong, I am well aware that after a loss, grief strikes when you don't expect it and I am well aware that the immediate feeling of loss can feel like you have entered the most awful black abyss in the world. But I am also completely aware, that I don't have to **be it**. There is no need for me to focus on my loss because it will turn up by itself in every memory, for any reason or for no reason.

So, this is my advice, you don't have to create a fixation on grief; its presence is strong enough. And to offset the pain and agony, I recommend that you change your focus by moving forward in every way. Learn everything you can about making a better life for yourself, your family, your friends, your occupation, your anything-at-all. Pick something you care about, change your focus to that and move forward anyway.

The pain will be there, so no need to entice it. Move forward. **What you place your focus on is your responsibility.** Let me be clear: there is no need to ignore your grief (that would be unhealthy). Please by all means feel your loss, but do not aggravate it. There is no need to listen to sad songs, read sad books or watch sad movies (I instinctually repelled all of these and still do), or engage voluntarily in any sad actions. Put all of that to the side, become a better person, love your lost one, feel your pain when it comes, and keep on moving forward.

Don't lay down and become your loss. Keep in mind that your loved one would never wish pain on you, so do push forward for your lost one, if you can't do it for yourself.

*"Grief starts to become indulgent, and it doesn't
serve anyone, and it's painful. But if you transform it into
remembrance, then you're magnifying the person you lost and also
giving something of that person to other people, so they can
experience something of that person."*
—Patti Smith

And always remember that your grief is a tribute to your love. If you didn't love that person so much, your grief would not be so heavy. **Love is the most beautiful feeling in the world and without it, yes, there would be no grief, but without it, there would be no life**. And realize this: your grief from loss will force you to gain your life like nothing else can. Unfortunately, there is no power greater than death that will give you life.

*"Grief is in two parts. The first is loss.
The second is the remaking of life."*
—Anne Roiphe

RECAP

You have now made the first Decision, "YES!!! I create my own reality!"

First, remember that your new word is YES! Say it out loud every morning! Say it again an hour later! Say it again every single hour! If you don't feel it, say it anyway! And YES! will now become your general approach to life. It is a powerful word and Mark Yarnell used it every single morning and all day long.

Making the YES! decision is so fundamental to extraordinary living that I want you to do the following for the next seven days: Keep *The Yarnell 7* by your side all day, every day, and open it to Chapter One, Decision One, "YES!" (If you are reading the ebook version or you run out of room here, go to the back of the book or go grab your free "Worksheets" at www.TheYarnell7.com

1. If you catch yourself with a negative thought: stop the thought, change it and then write it down like this:

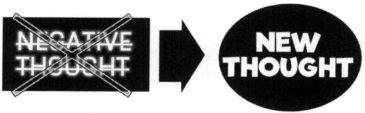

Day One:

Day Two:

Day Three:

Day Four:

Day Five:

Day Six:

Day Seven:

2. If you catch yourself with a negative reaction to anyone or any circumstance: stop it, change it and then write it down in here.

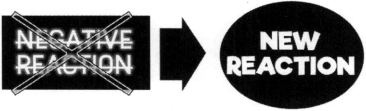

Day One:

Day Two:

Day Three:

Day Four:

Day Five:

Day Six:

Day Seven:

3. If you catch yourself having any feeling other than complete joy, happiness or peace: stop it, change it and write it down here.

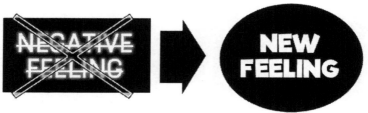

Day One:

Day Two:

Day Three:

Day Four:

Day Five:

Day Six:

Day Seven:

4. At the end of the day, review your progress, note your decisions to say "YES! I CREATE MY OWN REALITY," and give yourself a high five!

Decision One, done. Watch how everything changes now. Because once you make the **decision** to create your own reality in action and in perception, you have absorbed the number one dictator of your happiness. CONGRATULATIONS!

DECISION #2
ACTION!

"You can do anything that you really want to do."
—Mark Yarnell

Congratulations!

YES! You create your own reality and the next step is knowing you can do anything you want to do!

When I was a little girl about the age of five, I remember my dad picking me up and setting me up in his lap and saying to me, "You can do **anything** you really want to do." I paused and thought for a minute and my very five-year-old brain asked, "You mean, I can pick up a car?" He paused for a few seconds (and probably chuckled inside because only if you tell a child something so profound would you get a question like that). It didn't take very long for him to respond and his response would become very important in my life. He said, "I suppose if you really **wanted** to pick up a car, you could." And therein lies a very important distinction in the whole "You can do anything" debate of our time.

If you have been around and watched the news or the social "talk" in the last several years, you have heard commentators and writers bemoan the fact that parents, teachers and schools have been giving awards for everything a child does (or does not do). It doesn't matter if you win the race, you still get a medal for participation.

The general argument against this practice goes like this: by parents and teachers giving awards for everything and by telling their kids they can do anything, they have actually done a disservice to their children who now think they are entitled to awards for doing nothing. At the same time, they won't really do anything because they have no reason to try.

It is my supposition that medals and awards for participation are not a bad thing and that telling kids they can do anything is not a bad thing either. I was told that WAY before the generation of millennials. But what can be detrimental to development is leaving out that last clause "You can do anything **you really want to do**".

This is a huge distinction. What Dad did not say and what he did not "program" me with is "You can do anything, without doing anything!" Because to Mark Yarnell, that would be ridiculous. He believed in having goals, seeing those goals to fruition in your mind's eye, and taking the necessary actions to complete those goals. But he also believed that in order to do **anything**, you also must really want to do that thing; if you remove the "really want to" portion out of the phrase then you won't have the drive to actually complete the necessary actions to complete the goals.

> *I can teach anybody how to get what they want out of life. The problem is that I can't find anybody who can tell me what they want.*
> –Mark Twain

I found this to be a really interesting hurdle in my life because I enjoy doing all kinds of activities and I love to learn about a whole range of ideas and thoughts and concepts. Even when I was a little girl, I couldn't answer the question "What do you want to be?" I wanted to be one of each! Even though I have attained many, many goals, there are just as many that I haven't attained, not necessarily because I didn't have the skills, but because deep down inside, they simply weren't something I really wished to accomplish.

I recommend that when you create big goals that you take some sincere time and assess whether or not you truly want to achieve those goals. Sometimes we make goals that are unattainable, not because we aren't capable, but simply because they aren't authentically ours. It is easy to fool yourself into thinking that you want to do things because they seem like something you **should** do, not necessarily something that you truly desire. And there's a big difference. So save yourself some time and have a meaningful exchange with yourself about your honest desires. And then set your sights for what you want and go for it!

Let's go back: Decision One is YES! This is a general approach to life. This is the decision that you will make in the morning, throughout the day and before you go to bed. This is a decision to live a certain way, to be a certain way, and to create your own reality. That alone is huge but now add this to your YES bucket: You can do anything you really want to do!

You not only have the responsibility of perception and of defining your surroundings, but you also have the responsibility to then do anything you really want to do. This responsibility of saying yes to life through your actions is your next big decision and coupled with your newly developed awesome perceptions on everything, there is nothing that can hold you back!

So now, let's take some of your desires and let me show you how easy this really is:

You REALLY want to write a book? YES! WRITE IT!

You REALLY want to write songs and sing? YES! THEN SING THEM!

You REALLY want to own your own company? YES! THEN OWN IT!

You REALLY want a fantastic relationship with your significant other? YES! THEN CREATE IT!

And if you need some tools to help you complete your ACTIONS and get your desired result, please visit the "Resources" section at www.TheYarnell7.com

> *"Action is a great restorer and builder of confidence. Inaction is not only the result, but the cause, of fear. Perhaps the action that you will take will be successful; perhaps different action or adjustments will have to follow. But any action is better than no action at all."*
> —Norman Vincent Peale

When I was in my late thirties, I was ready for a career change because I love change … I really do! I was tired of traveling and wanted a bit of a rest. My then future husband wanted a career change too, as well as a nice rest from his busy traveling life. We also both wanted to move out of Tulsa and into a more beautiful environment, outside of the city. We moved to a lake and started brainstorming our next career moves.

Since his background is in the cosmetology industry and mine had most recently been in software within the cosmetology industry, he asked, "Why don't we just open a salon and boutique?"

And I thought for a moment and replied, "Okay! Where?"

He responded, "Why don't we just visit some of these smaller communities and pick one!"

I agreed and we decided in a matter of a week, leased a building and started painting. We opened six weeks later.

Here is the important part: we knew no one. Not one single person. But we had **decided** that this is what we really wanted to do next and so … we did it! We have never had one day that was not a success. We have never had one day when we didn't have a client in our salon and four years after we opened, we were voted Best Salon and my husband was voted Best Stylist by the community in the Daily Press's Best of Tahlequah annual vote.

Now remember, we did not know a single person in that community but we made a **decision to say yes** and then we developed a plan of ACTION and opened six weeks later! And because we really wanted a thriving salon and boutique, we created one.

Did it take work? YES! Did we succeed? YES.

WHY?

Because we really **wanted** to succeed.

Remember your mind is your responsibility. Your actions are your responsibility. Your decisions are your responsibility. And the beautiful thing is that you truly can do anything you really want to do. **The only boundaries are inside of your head.**

> *"Failure will never overtake me if my*
> *determination to succeed is strong enough."*
> —Og Mandino

When I was in my twenties, I was on a plane to go visit my dad and I was reading a health magazine that was in the seat pocket in front of me. Inside there was an advertisement for a "Before and After" type of health competition. I read it and while I was sitting right there on the plane, I decided to do it. Then because I really wanted to do well, I busted my butt in the gym and ate a body builder's menu. Twelve weeks later I had dropped a ton of weight and looked like a trophy. The transformation was unbelievable, even to myself. As a result, I ended up being in the Top Ten in my age bracket (out of something like 100,000+ people) and landed my before and after pictures in a best-selling book. Twenty years later I am still asked if that is me in the book … it is hilarious!

So here again, I said YES and had the belief that I create my own reality coupled with the fact that I **really wanted** to do it, (it took a whole lot of work) and so I succeeded.

When my dad was in his thirties, he joined his first network marketing company and started walking around telling everyone he met, "We are all gonna be RICH!" And guess what? Within a year, he had a pool and a beautiful house, was speaking to thousands of people and articles were being written about him. Why? Because he really wanted to be monetarily successful and he really wanted to have fun doing it! This was simply—drum roll please—a YES decision coupled with actions (and a ton of them!)

A few years later he decided he wanted to write a best-selling book and so, he did! And guess what? It became a best seller and he still earns royalties to this day, twenty-five years later. Do you know that it takes time and effort to write a book? But if you really want to do something… guess what, YES you can!

> *"Whatever the mind of man can
> conceive and believe, it can achieve."*
> —Napoleon Hill

You have made a decision to live an extraordinary life. And if you use *The Yarnell 7* every single day, you are bound to do so. Let's put what we have learned so far all together:

1. YES! You Create Your Own Reality:
   a. State it: In the morning and every hour (set a timer), say YES to yourself. Say it or think it with ENTHUSIASM!
   b. Catch & Change! When you catch yourself on the more negative end of the teeter-totter, CHANGE it and write it down in this book at the end of Decision #1 or on your worksheets from www.TheYarnell7.com. Review it tonight so you can give yourself kudos on being a Yarnell 7 "YES" person!

2. ACTION! You can do anything that you really want to do! So pretend you are a kid in a candy shop and look at all of those candies … now, ask yourself, what do you really want while you are here on Planet Earth? Write it down now and put it in your wallet. Look at it every single day and make a plan for each item. Okay, now ACT! Do it! Develop a plan and do it!

If for some strange reason, you feel stuck and you find yourself delaying the actions that you know you really should take, I suggest that you take a few minutes and think about the following:

We all know conceptually that we will get older and ultimately die. We all know that our regrets will not come in the form of what we did in life but what we did not do. Take a few minutes now and envision the end of your life and how you will truly feel if you do NOT take action on those goals that are important to you. Close your eyes and feel it. Now, take a moment to envision how you will feel if you accomplished that which you set out to do. Close your eyes and pretend that you have accomplished all of your goals, dreams, and desires. Do you feel the difference? Do you see how crucial it is to say YES and take action? **You must lead your life according to your major goals or you will find yourself in the future with the very same issues you have right now.** That kind of disappointment is completely unnecessary.

So, take ACTION! With the tools out there in our modern society, you don't ever have to be concerned that you don't know how to do something. All of that information is literally at your fingertips. And if your interests happen to align with some of mine, you can get great information from the "Resources" section at www.TheYarnell7.com!

FEAR:

FALSE EVIDENCE APPEARING REAL

Or

FORGET EVERYTHING AND RUN!

"Here we are traveling sixty-three thousand miles an hour on a tiny speck of dust we call Planet Earth toward 'God only knows' what peripheral reaches of the cosmos, and some people are worried about their pensions."
—Mark Yarnell

When dealing with physical fear or mental fear, you have two options. You can either see fear for what it is: nothing at all (False Evidence Appearing Real) OR you can succumb to fear, never do anything to combat it, run away fast and never live to the fullest (Forget Everything And Run). Fear is a strange beast. It is one thing to be scared because you think the boogieman is outside of your door because the boogieman really *is* outside of your door (call the police!) But it is a completely different beast when you are scared due to your own brain.

Oftentimes, fear feels like a logjam when it keeps us from moving on. What is even more annoying and crazy is that most fears are self-created prisons. They are based on absolutely nothing in reality. Interestingly enough, by facing very physical fears, we can break the bonds of many emotional or mental fears as well.

> *"Inaction breeds doubt and fear. Action breeds confidence and courage. If you want to conquer a fear, do not sit at home and think about it. Go out and get busy."*
> —Dale Carnegie

There are three important reasons to face fears in the physical realm:

1. Life is about experience, live it to the fullest!
2. Facing physical fears can destroy self-made fears.
3. Facing self-created, brain-made fears will take you to a higher level than you ever deemed possible.

About Experience:

Why would we be here if we weren't supposed to enjoy this world? Now, I am not saying you should go jump off a mountain in a paraglider because you need to experience it, but what I am saying is, if you are concerned about the second story in a mall because you can see the floor below you and therefore you avoid the mall when you actually love the mall, that's a problem. I am saying that if you look at the ocean or the lake and you know it is a beautiful world, made up of all kinds of incredible creatures and plants and wonderment but you don't feel like you are a strong swimmer (or have an irrational fear of the water), that's a problem. Any fear you have that stops you from experiencing your life is a problem that must be rectified immediately because ...

Your ability to face physical fears has a direct correlation with facing your internal fears. Facing physical fears will also help you to face mental and emotional fears. For some reason our brains can associate jumping off a mountain with self-worth, and that self-worth is important when facing your internal fears.

FREEDOM

"He who has overcome his fears will truly be free."
—Aristotle

Freedom and fear are polar opposites because fear will limit you and keep you from your own personal freedom. The number one trap that humans face is a lack of freedom based on self-imposed limitations. As you have read so far, there really are no limits. Just for a moment let's reflect on *The Yarnell 7* number one decision of YES. Yes means that you decide that you in fact do create your own reality based on your thoughts, perceptions and decisions. So let me ask you this? Do you have any fear of anything?

"You will never do anything in this world without courage."
—Aristotle

Fears of the physical hold you back in the mental and emotional realms too. So this is twofold: if you fear the water and never learn to swim, never experience the beauty of swimming and the life below the sea, you are just as apt to not face the fears inside that hold you back as well.

So if you do have any irrational fears of our physical world, then go ahead and face them.

"Exposure is hands down the most successful way to deal with phobias, anxiety disorders, and everyday fears of any sort."
—Phillippe Goldin, Stanford neuroscientist
Lifehacker, huffpost.com

Right now, go to your TY7 Worksheets or just grab a pen and make notes here:

What is your number one fear?

Commit to doing it anyway. What is the first step to combatting this fear?

Additional Steps:

Write your number one fear down and commit to doing it anyway. Take the first step as soon as you can. If the first step is to call someone to help then call someone who can help, today!

If you have a problem with swimming, call the nearest place with a swimming pool and ask how to take lessons or ask a friend who you trust to teach you. If you have a fear of heights, I would highly recommend that you go to the nearest high point in your city and look at the beauty of the city or land below you. Then you must repeat this process every single day until you feel fine about it.

Listen to me closely: remember YES! You create your own reality and take ACTION because you can do anything you really want to do! Remember that you are in control of your own thoughts and your own destiny so when your mind starts its never-ceasing activity of how scary heights or water or (name your fear here), catch it and stop it!

When I asked my dear Mum, Valerie (I call my dad's wife Mum because she is Canadian and I love the fact that I can call her Mum without encroaching on the title of my incredible, awesome biological Mom) and asked if she could send me a list of everything she associates with my dad, one of the things she shared with me is the following:

"He faced his fears head on and helped me do the same. That characteristic of courage influenced me greatly. I found myself stretching my boundaries—swimming, snorkeling, skiing out of bounds, sailing the British Virgin Islands during hurricane season, facing Grizzlies, holding a snake, paragliding, designing our home, and writing books."

So as you can see, freedom and fun were a big part of my dad's life and here's the deal: **in order to live life to the fullest, you must decide to do so.** Now, follow Decisions One and Two, face your fears both physical and mental, and you are really starting to live the The Yarnell 7 so that you can have an extraordinary life!

1. YES! you create your own reality
2. Take ACTION! You can do anything (you really want to do).
3. And remember, fear is a self-created prison that you must break out of starting now!

And here is the deal, when you have a fear that is keeping you from living life to the fullest, your natural inclination will be to say "but I don't truly *want* to do (this and such)." Trust me and do it anyway. That is just your irrational, fearful self, making the granddaddy of all lies. The easiest way to get out of doing something that you fear is to negate that the fear exists in the first place.

Now that we have remedied (and yes we have remedied them) the physical fears that you have, let's move on to the mental or self-created fears that you have.

FEAR of NO-THING

Human beings are such amazing creatures. Unlike any other creatures in the world, they have the ability to build boundaries that are completely unreal. They are based on absolute nothingness.

If you don't risk in life, you don't win in life because let's be real clear, there are no limitations except the ones you place on yourself. And the other amazing thing that humans can do, is make up excuses and actually trick themselves into believing their own lies! We are incredible! Talk about creating your own reality!

Oftentimes, we humans will make excuses that feel real, however, they are excuses that we use to mask our fear. Again, it is truly incredible that we are so adept at completely deceiving our own selves. Watch for the following excuses because you may be using them to hide your own fear from yourself and others!

The Granddaddy of all excuses: "I REALLY DON'T HAVE THE TIME!"

Truth: This is fear working on you! This is False Evidence Appearing Real! You are tricking yourself. (Isn't self-deception incredible?)

In 2016, a Nielson Company audience report revealed that adults in the United States dedicated about 10 hours and 39 minutes each day to consuming media. The report also showed that within that time, the average adult spends about 4.5 hours a day watching shows and movies.
According to a 2015 study by Common Sense Media, teens in the United States spend about nine hours a day using media for enjoyment. I know this sounds incredible and I am not sure how humans are pulling it off, but I am simply reporting the news.

Now, take a serious moment here, and just imagine what human beings would be capable of if they all decided to take away their gadgets. Just imagine our world if every single person dedicated nine hours of their day to making this world a better place. If everyone just took one hour of their precious time staring at a screen and worked on real-life issues such as social injustices and how to make this world a better place, the solutions that we could arrive at as a species would be incredible.

In fact, I implore you to institute an hour of each day with your family to do just that. Call it your TY7 hour and discuss together your action plans in your personal life and what you all can do to make this world a better place! We will discuss that in another chapter as well.

So again, when you (or your kids, who you are teaching by example) say, "I would love to do anything that I really want to do but I do not have the time!"

Repeat after me: "Rubbish rubbish RUBBISH! My time, my responsibility!"

This is what I do and what I do not do: I do not spend my time at night watching another TV program, another Netflix show, another movie. If I did, there would be no way for me to write this book. Instead, I choose to go to bed early and wake up early because I have a series of hours when I have undistracted time and can complete any project I really want to complete. Period.

So when you start the "I don't have the time" excuse, take a moment and ask yourself who is in charge of your time? Your kids? They sleep. Your job? It closes. This life is about you. You make your own decisions! You are an adult, right?

Just take anything you really want to do and see where you are using the time excuse.

Coincidentally, you will see it appearing with any part of self development: you want to write a book, write a song, lose weight, start exercising … pick one and just watch yourself playing the time game! When you use the oh-so-common words,

"I don't have the time," you should catch yourself and look at what fear you are trying to hide from yourself! If life is about living to the fullest and you create your own reality AND you can do anything you really want to do, then, what gives? If you honestly look at all of the hours you spend in mindless distraction, you will see that the time excuse is actually irrelevant.

And even if you really want to keep watching your shows on TV at night because that is the time you want to VEG (common excuse), then ...

Get up **one hour earlier** and start writing your book, singing your songs, studying that topic that will produce the results you really want to have and go for it! Take the risk! Live life to the fullest and stop it with the brain tricks!

> *"Take a chance. All life is a chance. The man who goes the farthest is generally the one who is willing to do and dare."*
> —Dale Carnegie

Let me tell you that time may be a reality in our world but time management is your reality; you create it. Do not play the "I don't have time" game with yourself or anyone else. If you really want to do something, then do it. Say YES! Take ACTION! And risk it! And let me tell you something else, there are plenty of resources out there to help you. Go to the Resources section of www.TheYarnell7.com (because chances are that you have the internet up and nearby you somewhere! BUSTED!).

Fear is life avoidance and 99.9 percent of the time you have made it up yourself. So from now on, when you say to yourself, "I would love to do that but I don't have the time," STOP. Realize what you are saying, which is essentially this: "I refuse to live an extraordinary life due to the fact that I need to watch television shows and read the incredible information on Facebook."

Do you really want to say that about your life? So when you hear the time excuse, stop it and change it and jot it down in the time section of this book or your worksheets. Catch yourself and change it. Really look at that statement and realize this: If you would really love to do something, go do it. Our timelines are based on our priorities.

TIME SECTION:

"I was kidding myself when I said I had no time! I said that about the following extraordinary goals, but I realize now that how I manage my time is my decision."

Make a time map of your day below.

Where are you spending your time? Make block segments below from the hour you get up to the hour you go to sleep:

My MORNING hours are from _____ to _____ and this is what I do:

My DAYTIME hours are from _____ to _____ and this is what I do:

My EVE & NIGHT-TIME hours are from _____to
_____and this is what I do:

Now, write down four goals for this year. Then write down your Top Three actions for each goal.

MY FOUR EXTRAORDINARY GOALS THIS YEAR ARE:

GOAL #1:

Action 1:

Action 2:

Action 3:

GOAL #2:

Action 1:

Action 2:

Action 3:

GOAL #3:

Action 1:

Action 2:

Action 3:

GOAL #4:

Action 1:

Action 2:

Action 3:

Now look back at the previous Time Map and mark out the time blocks that are senseless and re-write your new Time Map with your first three actions toward your four goals below. Every single day, review this Time Map/Goal/Action section and keep adjusting it accordingly by adding your new sets of actions toward the completions of your goals. (When this one gets overused, go to the back of the book for more space and also download new free ones in the "Worksheets" section at www.TheYarnell7.com) DO NOT DELAY. Make the decision to start RIGHT NOW. Go live an extraordinary life already!

NEW TIME MAP with ACTIONS toward GOALS:

My MORNING hours are from _____ to _____.

This is what I will do during those hours (Break the hours into smaller chunks):

From _____ to _____, I will:

From _____ to _____, I will:

From _____ to _____, I will:

My DAYTIME hours are from _____ to _____.

From _____ to _____, I will:

From _____ to _____, I will:

From _____ to _____, I will:

My EVE & NIGHT-TIME hours are from _____ to _____.

From _____ to _____, I will:

From _____ to _____, I will:

From _____ to _____, I will:

ONE MORE TIP: LEARN FROM OTHERS

When you are having a tough time creating your own reality and putting your dreams into action, learn from others. When you recognize that your life is your responsibility but for some strange reason, you feel like you are stuck in your own perceptions and you are having a hard time creating the extraordinary life that you deserve, one of the best things you can do for yourself is to take the time to read about and watch movies and videos about those human beings who have overcome extraordinary hardships to live extraordinary lives.

There are many human beings who serve as inspirational reminders to us if we look for them.

When we take the time to step out of our own realities and to look at others, many times we will find that push we need to take the actions necessary for our growth. Other people have stories that will propel you to new levels. Always remember that if one human being can do it, so can you.

FIND YOUR EDNA!

After Dad died, I started reading everything I could about life after death and any other thing I could find to make myself feel like I was closer to him. After about a year of that, I realized that I needed to switch my focus and make some real headway as a person. And then along came Edna.

We have all heard that "when the student is ready, the teacher will appear." I had never experienced this and always wanted to and then boom, it happened! If you ever have the opportunity to spend time with someone who truly lives an extraordinary life, don't walk, RUN to that person!

After almost a year of pain and trying to make my life better, I was absolutely empowered by spending time with Edna. She lives in a world of peak performance; she has a business coach, she is engaged in mastermind communities, she thinks positively. Edna does more real estate transactions in one year than most real estate agents do in five years or more—in fact, in 2016 she was the number eight real estate agent at Century 21 in the entire United States and we live in a county where the average sales price of a home is $100,000!

What I have gained from working with her and spending time with her is absolutely immeasurable. When our schedules are completely full, she winks at me and says, "Ya know what, Amy? This is a really great problem to have!" Two to three times a week when I walk into her office, she looks up from her desk, hands on her keyboard and all of the sudden with a sly grin, the room is filled with dance music emanating from her computer and you know what? WE DANCE! Right there in her office, we dance! Because, why not? If you are going to choose to work hard, you might as well have an awesome time doing it!

If you ever have the chance to be around someone who is at the top of their game, do it. Your life will change forever because those people, even if they don't say it or know it themselves, already live *The Yarnell 7*. If you spend time around them, your life will rise to incredible heights! This is why it is very important for you to align with other TY7 Decision Makers. Being surrounded by people who constantly create their own realities and are aware of the fact that they can do anything they really want to do, creates a synergy of sorts that is absolutely unstoppable!

A really good way to figure out how to find your Edna is to decide what you want to do next and then to look for the leaders in that field. From real estate agents to writers to speakers and entrepreneurs, you will find that many of these incredible high performers are actually quite accessible. In fact, I remember my dad contacting many authors who had written books that he found extraordinary just so he could learn from them. Look for the top of the top and contact them. Leave a voicemail or send an email and simply tell them you want to learn from them. You will find that many outstanding individuals who lead extraordinary lives are happy to help you do the same. So go

FIND YOUR EDNA ... surround yourself by examples of *The Yarnell 7* and watch your life grow exponentially!

DECISION #3

RESPONSIBILITY

"The extent to which you are willing to accept responsibility for your own voyage will ultimately dictate the fulfillment you experience when your achievements have been realized."
—Mark Yarnell

You are well on your way to living an extraordinary life, because you now know that your perceptions and your actions are just that, yours. (That's a whole lot of freedom right there!)

Now let's take it one step further, your perceptions and your actions are your responsibilities. Gone are the days of excuses and gone are the days of whining. You simply cannot point at other people and decry that your life is a result of their behavior because you have complete control of your life. And so repeat after me:

"MY LIFE, MY RESPONSIBILITY."

There is no greater freedom than realizing that your life is your own. But once it truly sinks in, you must look at it as your responsibility. This is when it gets really serious: you can no longer point the finger anywhere but at yourself.

Does that bother you? The only times that this will bother you are when you really don't care for your own reality. But even if that is the case, you must take responsibility for it. There is no one else you can look to and there is nowhere else to point. Now, you know from the YES decision that your perception of your life around you is the definition that you give every single element of your life.

So, ask yourself this, "When am I willing to relinquish my excuses and really take control of my life?"

COMMON TRAPS

Because you already have YES & ACTIONS down, let's look at some common traps that you actually create to protect yourself. Traps occur when you try to negate your responsibility to your own self. Human beings will try very hard to create traps to protect themselves when they feel limited but also feel like they don't have control. You also create traps when you simply don't want to be accountable for your life or life decisions.

Self-Created Trap #1: I am a victim of my past.

"The past is a place of reference, not a place of residence;
the past is a place of learning, not a place of living."
—Roy T Bennett

This is a very common trap and in order to live an extraordinary life, you must free yourself from it.

This will NOT work: *Yes! I create my own reality and I can do anything BUT my mom was a real jerk and as a result, there is some kind of amorphous self-sabotage beast that swoops in on my life and takes me fourteen steps backward on any given day. It is really hard to succeed because my mom treated me poorly!*

Cut it out already. Take RESPONSIBILITY. Your mom may have been a real jerk but this is in the past. If you are basing your life on anything in the past, you are basing your life on nothing at all because the past is gone! And there is no beast called self-sabotage.

Take this moment and write down two things in your past that you tend to point at as reasons for your lack of extraordinary behavior.

POINTS IN THE PAST:

1.

2.

Now: cross them out. I want you to put a big, bad X over each one right now. Next: take a loose piece of paper and write down something that happened in your past that you point to as an excuse for your lack of extraordinary living. Now rip it up into tiny little pieces and throw it in the trash can! This is your life, not your mom's, not your dad's, not your Aunt Tilly's so throw the past away!

You only have NOW and if you are having a problem wrapping your brain around this one, take a moment to realize that any person who harmed you in the past, did not know about *The Yarnell 7* and was mindlessly reacting to his or her own life. And listen to this: if you were in their shoes, you would have done exactly the same thing.

Do you understand this? Think about it. If you were actually in another person's shoes, you would act and behave the same way. Give them all a break. They are humans, they messed up, not your circus, not your monkeys. Move on down the road!

YES! I create my own reality and YES! I can do anything I really want to do.

Now, repeat after me:

MY LIFE! MY RESPONSIBILITY!

Got it? Good.

I do realize that touching on the past may be harsh for some of you who experienced horrible loss, tragedy or abuse in your former years. It may sound a bit callous of me to say move on so let me just throw a little caveat out there: I, of course, think it is awful and horrifying that any kids are mistreated by their parents or guardians and I am deeply sympathetic for anyone who was born into any hardship from their external realities. And if you are struggling or exhibiting signs of mental illness or emotional instability, I am absolutely for you seeking counseling or psychiatric help.

But with that, I have to remind you, that as an adult this is also your responsibility. If you are unable to throw the past away and start anew, then you have to seek help right now. You have to move on, but you don't have to move on alone. And once you have, I am a firm believer that some of the most beautiful and fantastic gifts we can receive in this world of ours are from people who have been through horrible pain. Pain makes human beings more empathetic to other people and if they can move beyond their own pain, the gifts that they have for the world are unsurpassed.

Please consider that your hardships can be your gifts and you can offer those to everyone else and nurture others so that they too can live extraordinary lives! (More on nurturing in the next chapter!)

"The most beautiful people we have known are those who have known defeat, known suffering, known struggle, known loss, and have found their way out of those depths."
—Elisabeth Kubler-Ross

If you grew up in an awful environment or experienced harsh conditions as a child or in a former relationship, that is indeed awful, especially when you are young and you really have no way out of the situation. But you still have to let go, for your sake and for the sake of everyone else who will learn from your existence. It doesn't matter if you let go by going to see a counselor or you simply make a decision to let go, you still have to let go. And you have to do this for two reasons: one, so that you can live an extraordinary life and two, so that you can share your free self and who you are with others so that they can receive the help they need as well.

"Out of suffering have emerged the strongest souls; the most massive characters are seared with scars."
—Khalil Gibran

"Character cannot be developed in ease and quiet. Only through the experience of trial and suffering can the soul be strengthened, ambition inspired, and success achieved."
—Helen Keller

So, to all of you out there who have lived difficult or even horrible childhoods or have experienced incredible pain, your responsibility is even greater. You not only have the responsibility to release the past and grow, but your growth is exactly what the rest of the world needs because your gifts to the world can be the greatest gifts we can receive!

THE POWER OF WORDS

Common Trap #2: It is someone else's fault that I am feeling this way!

Any time you think or utter the words "Someone else made me _____ (insert the negative feeling here)," catch yourself and stop it!

No one can **make** you feel anything! It is impossible! Any time you actually say those words or any string of words that places the reasons for how you are feeling on someone else, catch yourself and change it!

Remember the story about my dad when he refused to acknowledge that I might make him feel excited while he was on his literal deathbed? Making the decision to accept complete responsibility of your life is essential to your growth and to your main objective which should be to live an extraordinary life. It is a debilitating habit to give anyone else power over your own feelings and it is also simply a mistaken perspective.

The other day, I was talking with one of my employees who wanted to discuss with me why she was upset the previous day at work. And though I was proud of her for acknowledging the uncomfortable situation, she used the two most common excuses for her behavior. One was a habitual way of speaking that many people adopt: "I was trying to figure out why you made me so mad yesterday."

First, I can't **make** anyone mad and you can't **make** me mad!

Then, she laid down the next whopper for me: "It is because when I was young, my mom mentally tortured me."

So now, I have an unhappy employee because she has equated her past with her present and ALL of it is actually her mom's fault. Now listen carefully, this young woman is bright and beautiful. I do not doubt that her mom made some pretty hefty mistakes and I also do not doubt that when my employee is reminded of her past by something that happens in the present that she will have a strong and immediate reaction to present circumstances.

The key here is to do what my employee did, but to do it quickly: Catch those reactions, nullify them with understanding, and let them go as quickly as possible. Again, if you can catch your visceral reactions to the present, realize that they are from the past (like she did), and then drop them, move on, and let it go, you have succeeded!

Catching yourself, acknowledging the confusion and moving on down the road is success because you have let go of the past and returned to the present, where all of your reality is yours! Plus, your future reactions will have less punch because you have realized that the past is not the present and that this life and time is yours!

And remember the power of words. Any time you hear yourself give any power over to another human being regarding your life, catch yourself, write it down, change it and move on. Listen for these types of phrases either in your head or coming out of your mouth:

"He makes me so mad."

"I was having a great day and then she …"

"I try to give to my relationship but he makes me crazy."

"I want to live an extraordinary life but my boss sucks the life out of me!"

My friends, these are all excuses and not only that, they are habitual excuses. These excuses are absolutely catastrophic in terms of you living an extraordinary life. They take the responsibility away from yourself, which is absolutely impossible. You are in charge of you!

And once we know about this game, it is liberating. Take your excuse and mark it out. Now write down the opposite of the excuse. Here is an example:

"Henry hurt my feelings."

~~"Henry hurt my feelings."~~

"I allowed myself to feel pain when Henry mentioned my report to our coworker."

Resolution: Either "I realize that I need to change my report because I can do better and Henry's not-so-nice comment reminded me that I can do better." OR "I like my report and that's what matters!"

Make it a mantra, make it a song if you have to, but keep repeating "MY LIFE, MY RESPONSIBILITY!" throughout the day, like a chorus in your head. Now smile, because isn't it truly wonderful to know that it all comes down to you?

The Habit of Complaint

"NO WHINING!"
—Mark Yarnell

Human beings are such interesting creatures. Have you ever noticed that when you ask a friend or an acquaintance or even a complete stranger how they are doing, that the response is 90 percent negative? The complaints are endless!

"How am I? Well, my boss, ugggggh. She is just AWFUL. Today she …"

"I am just ready for this weather to pass … it is so dreary!"

"I am doing pretty well but my son is about to send me over the edge!"

I cannot begin to figure out why humans get so stuck on the down side of the teeter-totter of happiness. Even though elimination of the teeter-totter is inevitable as a TY7 Decision Maker, it is still hard to resist a good complaint because they are used as bonding tools between humans. We tend to commiserate with one another about the annoyances of the day. And as a TY7 Decision Maker, you will find it strange that when you offer something that is upbeat in response to the incessant negativity, sometimes the complainer can't even hear it! They just continue as if you haven't said anything at all … but don't give up on spreading the happiness.

As a person who is now well on your way to living an extraordinary life, I implore you to change this habit within yourself. If someone asks you how your day was, you either respond with "FANTASTIC" or you respond with something specific like, "it was great because …" I know that the more we focus on what is awesome collectively as a species, the better things will be.

> *"Be grateful for what you have and stop complaining—it bores everybody else, does you no good, and doesn't solve any problems."*
> —Zig Ziglar

So today, choose to be a leader in the TY7 campaign for extraordinary living and stop the whining! If you catch yourself coming up with a complaint to commiserate with the human species, catch it and write it down in the worksheets in the back of this book. Now, verbally, say something positive at the end. "I can't stand this weather" turns into "I can't stand this weather but it was still a great day and I know it will be beautiful outside soon!"

Another really awesome tool when you are in the habituated state of commiserative complaining is to verbally (and internally) note that the bad makes the good! For example, "I know, Hilda, this weather is awful but what I do love is the fact that the crappy weather makes beautiful weather seem even more beautiful!" This is similar to giving your past the recognition of the fact that without it, you wouldn't have become the fabulous human being you are. You can do this with almost everything, "My boss is a real jerk but she has taught me so much about how to be a better leader!" When you start a complaint, recognize the good that comes out of the situation.

If you are small talking with someone and they launch a whole lot of complaints, simply smile and nod and when you can, offer some good thoughts to the other person. If they actually give you time to talk in between their incessant chatter of negativity, take it and add all of the positive ways that they could change their lives!

If they don't offer a pause in their stream of negative speaking, eventually they may still stop and ask you how your day is going. Now, if that happens, you really have the opportunity to shine! And the great news is, when you shine, so will they! It goes like this:

Bob: "And then she went behind my back and told the others!"

You just shake your head and roll your eyes (you are commiserating and being human … but you keep a slight smile).

You allow a pause in the conversation because the other person will eventually catch themselves and they will realize that they should probably stop their stream of consciousness (or not-so-consciousness), and they will ask you how your day was … YES! Now you have the opportunity to help turn it all around!

Bob: "Enough about my crappy day, how is yours going?"

You: "My day is AWESOME! I really enjoy this weather and my coworkers are incredible people and I am working on an amazing project right now outside of work!"

Then they may or may not engage in conversation about your awesome life but either way, at least you contributed to happiness rather than everything other than happiness. Nice work! Record that in your notes too! This can become an incredible habit and you will see it in TY7 leaders, but more on that later.

"If you took one-tenth the energy you put into complaining and applied it to solving the problem, you'd be surprised by how well things can work out … Complaining does not work as a strategy. We all have finite time and energy. Any time we spend whining is unlikely to help us achieve our goals. And it won't make us happier."

—Randy Pausch

The Last Lecture

Now, today (and every day), catch yourself in an excuse. Any excuse at all. You can catch yourself using words that deny your own responsibility and your own power, or you can catch yourself excusing your current emotions and behaviors based upon your past which is now over. Or you can catch yourself in the habitual "complaint world of commiseration"! The key is catch and change!

As the day moves forward, keep *The Yarnell 7* open to the "Responsibility" worksheet in the back of this book and write down any defeating words you have used today. Then, write next to your excuse, how it doesn't cut the mustard. Call yourself on your own bull*%$#. And then, laugh about it. If you managed to stop the powerless words that you used or you managed to help someone else do that just by being an example, write it down and celebrate!

A note on authenticity: at first you may question everything in this book, as I once did, by asking the question, "If I am upbeat and happy all of the time, am I living an authentic life? What about the feelings that aren't so happy and upbeat? Aren't those feelings valid? Don't we talk to each other about these problems to bond as human beings and get feedback from one another?"

Yes, they are valid because when something bothers you or when a problem is presented in your life, you can take that opportunity to ask yourself, "Okay, what is the problem here and how do I solve it?" Then you can take the applicable Yarnell 7 decisions and apply them to that problem. But the point here is that you solve it, you don't become it.

This is similar to grief and illness. There are real problems in life and they stimulate feelings that aren't so awesome but let those feelings act as reminders that you have an opportunity for growth. Feel them then release them, and move on to the exciting parts of being able to solve them. These difficult emotions serve a really wonderful purpose because uncomfortable feelings or problems are fantastic solution-opportunities and without them, well, we would be somewhat stunted.

Talking with your close friends and family to ask for help in finding a solution is one thing but spreading your negative feelings to everyone else by habitually complaining, is another thing altogether. Think of it as the flu. You don't ever want to spread the flu, right? But thoughts can be like the flu too; negativity is contagious and you simply must choose not to spread it!

So about authenticity: even as a member of *The Yarnell 7* Decision Makers, you will have "down" moments but what is important here is that they need only be moments. They don't need to be days and then weeks and then months and then years and then the next thing you know, your whole life.

So, if you are feeling blue, note the feeling and look at the cause. Now, go solve the problem and live an extraordinary life! YOUR LIFE, YOUR RESPONSIBILITY! YES!

DECISION #4

NURTURE

"You MUST have a goal bigger than yourself."
—Mark Yarnell

To nurture others is a fundamental decision in *The Yarnell 7* way of life because unless you give to other individuals as well as to the collective group of humanity, you run the risk of feeling a great void, a hole, a missing piece.

Because honestly, if the end game of your life doesn't make the world a better place, then what gives?

Think about it: if you approach the world with YES! and know that you create your own reality and you also decide that you are the epitome of ACTION because you can do anything you really want to do and you couple that with the understanding that your life is your RESPONSIBILITY, then what about everyone else?

You can speak, act, sing, own a business, be the best at your workplace, create a beautiful family and all of this is absolutely wonderful but until you decide to NURTURE others and create a goal bigger than yourself, you are missing out on the rest of the world and you can't possibly live a truly extraordinary life!

When I was beginning to outline this book, I wanted to get ideas from other people about how they felt about Mark Yarnell and so I asked our contacts on Facebook to submit their Yarnell stories. The beautiful outcome of this was that almost everyone wrote a Nurture story. Of course, they sent me hilarious stories too but for the most part, they were stories about how my dad had helped them become better people. Mark Yarnell took the time to help nurture other people in business as well as in their personal lives. His constant attention to nurturing others was truly inspiring.

You have been given the opportunity (especially if you are living *The Yarnell 7*) to nurture other human beings and to help them grow and contribute and live extraordinary lives! Now I don't mean you can nurture others by handing them this book (though it certainly wouldn't hurt), what I mean is that you have to actually help other human beings, for the sake of yourself and for the sake of them.

> *"It is literally true that you can succeed best*
> *and quickest by helping others to succeed."*
> —Napoleon Hill

Take a moment to reflect on life and all that is important to you, new careers, fancy cars, houses, great relationships and now, place it in your mind's eye that you have attained all of those goals. Now ask yourself, what else? And you **will** ask yourself that question because after you reach all of your goals, you will wonder what that void you feel inside is … that void is the intrinsic knowledge that there is something more … and that "more" is other people! You must nurture the world and make it a better place. **At all times, remember this, the world needs you.**

Nurture Individuals

> *"Beginning today, treat everyone you meet as if they were going*
> *to be dead by midnight. Extend to them all the care, kindness*
> *and understanding you can muster, and do it with no thought*
> *of any reward. Your life will never be the same again."*
> —Og Mandino

Start with the individual; start by listening. Listen well and then when someone has an idea or a desire or a wish to live a better life, be a better person, make this world a better place, I want you, as a Yarnell 7 decision-making human being, to take a moment and encourage that person. Encourage them and expand them.

This actually makes for a great day: listen to what others are saying and then pretend they are plants and take your proverbial water and help them grow.

For example, when a person at your place of work (or place of fun) discusses a story that she saw on the news last night about poverty and hunger in the downtown area of your town, acknowledge it and then ask: did the news provide a solution or a way we can help?

Now, take the answer from your friend and encourage him or her to let you know what the solution is and help him expand the solution. Make it a discussion. This is a great way to make the world a better place one person at a time!

Similarly, if your friend is talking to you in the break room and mentions that she wishes she was a writer because she has a great idea for a book, smile big (because you know the secret of creating your own reality and the fact that you can do anything) and nurture her with encouragement. Contribute your own ideas on how she would go about doing that!

Even if you don't have a foggy clue about what the other person is talking about and how to do it, discuss the power of information technology.

Just say this: "That is an AWESOME idea and you should do it!"

Your coworker might chuckle with the common "Yeah, right," or she may say "You really think I should?"

Say, "No, I am serious!" or "ABSOLUTELY, you really should! I have no idea how you would go about doing that but that is why I so love the Internet! We are incredibly lucky to be able to find out so much in five minutes. Thirty years ago, you would have had to talk to people and go to the library to figure out how to do stuff but now fifteen minutes of Google can really change things!"

Now look, in five minutes (five minutes!), you have listened and nurtured another human being. And the most awesome thing about that small nurturing action is that the person may actually make a move toward writing a book. Later, she or he may tell this story of the break room and she or he will also be more likely to encourage others which means the nurturing becomes contagious. How is that for contribution?

When you listen and nurture other humans, you are creating a better world and you will notice how wonderful they feel as a result. Sometimes the person you are talking to has never received even the slightest amount of encouragement and so getting even a bit from a coworker in a break room, is a huge deal!

I am amazed at how people react when I simply listen and then nurture their ideas ... sometimes it is so foreign to the person that they don't even hear what I am saying for a minute. When they start to catch on and then when they finally get it, I can physically see their faces changing into something softer and more real. Just this one small contribution can change the planet!

Of course, it goes without saying, that you nurture your friends and family as well. Every single person who you can nurture, decide to do it! This can take an extra thirty seconds or an extra fifteen minutes of your day and if you are really absorbed in the idea, it may take a lunch or dinner but who cares ... you both just grew as people! You are making the TY7 decision to NURTURE other humans and they all deserve it.

BY NURTURING OTHERS, YOU ARE NURTURING YOURSELF.

"In our heart of hearts, beyond our personal needs, most of us find life much more gratifying when we help others."
—Mark Yarnell

When you give, you grow. Today, listen for ideas, listen for problems, ask questions, and then offer suggestions (even if you don't know any, Google is a great suggestion!) Do it every single day. In the Nurture section in the back of this book, today and every day from here on out, write about who you nurtured and how. Make it a decision in every single encounter to listen for the ideas and desires of others and then grow them.

Making the decision to nurture other people (outside of your norm of family and friends) is definitely a goal bigger than yourself but let's take this one step further.

Nurture the World

When you make *The Yarnell 7* decisions and you know that you create your own reality and that you can do anything, and that your life is your responsibility, you will change ... and I mean a lot. Suddenly, you will be singing and dancing around by yourself, you will be way more effective, you will be building a truly extraordinary life but listen closely, you must have a goal bigger than yourself. This is nurturing on a collective basis.

One day, my dad and I were sitting on the porch off of my bedroom at his house in Reno and we were talking about how awesome it was that he was able to cut a check to The United Way for $150,000. We were talking about the whole philosophy of what you give, you receive. This fundamental truth becomes extremely obvious when you incorporate nurturing others both individually and collectively. He looked at me with a slight smile and said, "It's just a strange realization because you can't help feeling a little selfish when you give with the knowledge that you will receive so much back." We both laughed at the strangeness of it all, but it is so true.

You think I am crazy but trust me when I say that this DECISION to have a goal bigger than yourself is fundamental to your success as a human being and if you lack this decision, you are going to lose your momentum in life. There are only so many trips you can take, so many houses you can buy, so many fabulous outfits you can wear, so many incredible meals you can have and so many fabulous businesses you can be a part of, before you ask yourself "Is this all there is?" And when people get to that point, they tend to sabotage themselves; they stop growing, stop learning, stop expanding, stop being extraordinary.

Why do you think so many people who seemingly have great lives and have nailed all three of the preceding Yarnell 7 decisions (think: actors and singers and writers), make decisions that completely ruin their lives? When a person reaches all of the obvious worldly goals and he or she isn't prepared with the knowledge that to live a truly extraordinary life he or she must nurture others, life suddenly looks hollow and meaningless. It is a very dangerous place to reach and in their search for fulfillment, when they have reached the height of their careers, they give up everything they have due to the realization that they have nothing at all.

"We make a living by what we get.
We make a life by what we give."
—Winston S. Churchill

WHAT CONCERNS YOU MOST ABOUT OUR WORLD?

Make it a decision today to brainstorm what matters to you in this world. Do you feel concerned for people who are starving? Does it worry you that people have mental illness issues or addiction problems? Are you bothered that some people have a lack of good water in their communities? What is it, in this world, that you want to solve?

Write your list here:

Now, look at your list. You now have one or more things that truly irk you about our world. The next step is to do something about it. It doesn't matter how big or small your goal is, because all movements toward making this world a better place count. Do not skip this decision.

I once saw a man take the stage in front of hundreds of people to share his experience of going to different third world communities to dig wells on behalf of a very large rotary group. This rotary club had raised a lot of funds to drill water wells so that communities in other countries could have good, clean water without walking miles and miles away from home.

This man was born and raised here in the United States and lived a seemingly normal life but he was given the opportunity and made the decision to go to these places and procure the necessary equipment to drill these wells. The rotary members asked him to take the stage and as hundreds of rotary members were watching him from their tables, he walked up to the microphone and paused. Then, guess what he did? He cried. He didn't say much. He cried.

The tears were not born of sadness but instead the tears were born of beauty. He had lived a goal bigger than himself and he was so incredibly grateful to have meaningfully touched thousands of lives and to have seen first-hand how these other people lived and how happy and joyous they were over **receiving a water supply**. There was a film with people from these communities literally dancing in the water that sprung from the well. Talk about relativity.

For 99.9 percent of the people reading this book, I can say with 100 percent certainty, we have no excuses for not living extraordinary lives. Absolutely zero. We have food, we have water, we have shelter, we are free to do what we choose to do with no hindrances. The only hindrances are self-created.

We have the responsibility to not only nurture other human beings within the realms of our experiences here in the world but we also have the responsibility to help other human beings by taking massive action.

Trust me on this: You make a goal bigger than yourself and watch the whole world grow.

The Starfish Story

Once upon a time, there was an old man who used to go to the ocean to do his writing. He had a habit of walking on the beach every morning before he began his work. Early one morning, he was walking along the shore after a big storm had passed and found the vast beach littered with starfish as far as the eye could see, stretching in both directions.

Off in the distance, the old man noticed a small boy approaching. As the boy walked, he paused every so often and as he grew closer, the man could see that he was occasionally bending down to pick up an object and throw it into the sea. The boy came closer still and the man called out, "Good morning! May I ask what it is that you are doing?"

The young boy paused, looked up, and replied, "Throwing starfish into the ocean. The tide has washed them up onto the beach and they can't return to the sea by themselves. When the sun gets high, they will die, unless I throw them back into the water."

The old man replied, "But there must be tens of thousands of starfish on this beach. I'm afraid you really won't be able to make much of a difference."

The boy bent down, picked up yet another starfish and threw it as far as he could into the ocean. Then he turned, smiled and said, "It made a difference to that one!"

Adapted from *The Star Thrower* by Loren Eiseley (1969)

The Starfish Story never gets old to me. If you really think about making the world a better place, and you start to feel that the problems are too big and overwhelming, remember that each person counts. It doesn't matter if you help a million people or you help one person. Every person counts.

Do not move forward in *The Yarnell 7* without deciding how you are going to do this one thing. Because in order to live truly extraordinary lives, we must nurture others as individuals and as a collective whole. It is up to us. Every single one of us.

DECISION #5

ENTHUSIASM

*"Stand with your feet firmly planted and SHINE
YOUR LIGHT. There are people searching for it."*
—Mark Yarnell

Mark Yarnell always bounced. His walk was strong and his posture was tall. He walked mightily at his house (you could hear him everywhere he went) and in public, in the wee morning hours and at 7 p.m. His enthusiasm for life was incredible. Why? How? He had accomplished so many things and been to so many places that every now and then, I felt like a puppy cocking my head to the side with confusion because I wondered how he was able to maintain that degree of excitement.

One day, on the phone, I was feeling kind of low and I equated my lack of enthusiasm to a feeling of boredom inside, a certain monotony with life and so I asked him, "Dad, you have done everything, you have been everywhere, you have experienced so much, how is it that you are still so excited all the time?"

He paused for just a few seconds and then as if he was giving me a recipe for meatballs over the phone, he said:

"Okay here is what I do: I make plans to do things that I love to do. For example, on Wednesday night I know I am going to go over to eat at Momo Sushi. I LOVE SUSHI! Then on Friday there is a new movie coming out that can't wait to see, so on Friday, Valerie and I are going to go see it! And on Saturday, you know what I am going to do? I am going to go paragliding with the guys! So, honey, here is what you do: you simply make plans to go do the things you LOVE to do, no matter how big or how small, and all week, every week you look forward to them!"

It seemed so simple but as it is with many simple concepts, it was quite profound. What Dad was really saying was this: I choose the little things that I enjoy and then I blow them so far up (some people would say out of proportion) and I make them so big and then I decide to be crazy excited! I am then the quintessential enthusiastic person because **that is how I choose to live.**

Now, this was most definitely a decision on his part. Think about it: his whole adult life, the man had done anything and everything he wanted to do: he traveled to Europe, he traveled to Japan, he sailed the Virgin Islands, he spoke to thousands of people, he wrote best-selling books, he jumped off of mountains, he owned mansions and awesome cars and he had everything in the material world that he wanted to have and not only that, he had accomplished goals much bigger than himself. He had a prison program, he had donated to the United Way, he had nurtured tons of individuals and monetarily backed them on their ideas … so what gives?

Even at the time of that conversation I realized this was a big AHA moment for me but what I didn't ask him about his sushi plans and his movie plans was, how do you take something so small and make it so big? Of course, I know how. He made a decision to be excited. That's all.

The decision to be enthusiastic is incredibly vital to living *The Yarnell 7* because it is a feeling inside and it is a feeling that is projected on the outside where other people can catch it like an enthusiasm airborne virus. Let's take a moment and reflect on the power of decisions. When you think of an emotion, most of the time, you will think of it as something that just happens and yes, if you let all your emotions be reactions to your life's circumstances, then emotions are very reactionary. But as you now know from *The Yarnell 7*, everything is a choice and this includes your level of enthusiasm.

The BESTS!

We've all heard the saying "Let's not make mountains out of molehills!" And when we are talking about problems or issues or fears, I totally agree. But when we are talking about positive things, let's do it ... let's take a molehill and make it a mountain!

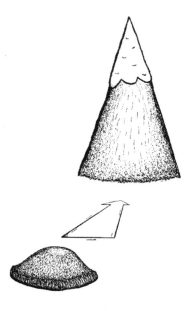

Here's another example of molehills to mountains: everything in Dad's life was the "best thing ever." Mum, Christine, Eric and I would laugh out loud knowing what was going to happen at the dinner table. If someone cooked him a steak, it was the BEST

FILET MIGNON EVER! If he cooked fried potatoes with his meal the very next night, they were the BEST POTATOES EVER! If it was a beautiful day outside, it was THE BEST DAY EVER! So, every day, all of the beauty in his life, was the BEST EVER! Of course, what is really interesting about that, is that it can't be refuted. At that moment, it was the BEST to him ... how can you argue with that?

How do you make a decision to be excited? The same way you make a decision to go to work today. The same way you decide to wear the navy blue shirt. The same way you decide to take a shower. You do it the same way we have discussed in every chapter preceding this. It is interesting to think about this concept in terms of passion.

One time, I was listening to Tony Robbins who is the tool master behind powerful living via psychological and physiological tools and one of the questions I had been struggling with was "What am I truly passionate about?" I was in the wake of Dad's death and I was feeling very mediocre about everything so passion was a missing element. One of Tony's CD's hit on this very topic and reflected, in concept, how my dad had chosen to live. In fact, Tony's very tagline is "Live with Passion!"

And guess what? That's a decision again. You decide to be passionate. You dictate your passion and enthusiasm. You bring it; you don't wait for it to arrive. You decide to live an exciting life. You walk like it and you talk like it and guess what, life is suddenly exciting!

EXCITEMENT TOOLS

So, each and every day make a conscious effort to remember these tools:

First, remember **YES!** You create your own reality.

Second, remember **ACTION!** You can do anything you really want to do!

Third, remember to repeat "My life, My **RESPONSIBILITY!**"

Fourth, repeat the mantra for **NURTURE!**: "I am making the world a better place!"

Now I even get excited every time I think of those four things by themselves but here are some additional tools so that you keep up your level of **EXCITEMENT!**

Physical Strength

Sit up, stand straight, and walk strong.

Any time you catch yourself slouching, sit up. When you are standing, straighten up. And when you walk, walk strong. This sounds so simple I know, but try it right now. Today, all day, let this be your being mantra: sit up, straighten up, walk strong! Do it, you will be amazed.

From Molehills to Mountains

Make small, BIG.

Take the smallest things that you enjoy, put them on the calendar, and make them huge. Again, this is a decision. Remember when I told you that less than twenty-four hours after Dad passed away, I looked out at his lake view from his office and thought, "HE DID IT." He lived an extraordinary life, by choice. All the way through it!

You can either think, "Yeah yeah, dinner on Thursday night at the Chinese restaurant."

OR you can think, "WOOHOOO! THIS THURSDAY NIGHT I GET TO GO TO ASIAN STAR WITH MY AWESOME FRIENDS!"

See that? Yes, it is all in your mind, as usual. So right now, I want you to choose one activity and put it into your calendar in the next seven days. Schedule it and take that one thing that is small and make it big!

What awesome activity will you schedule in the next seven days? Remember, you can schedule more than one; but either way, put them in your calendar!

CRANK UP THE TUNES!

This was a real biggie for my dad. When iTunes came along, the world shifted in the Mark Yarnell house because he figured out that he could purchase every single song that excited him. This was so important to him that the last time I saw him awake I tried to give me his iPad so I could listen to his songs that very night!

His playlist consisted of all the songs from his youth that made him feel happy. There is not a single sad song in his selection. All of them are upbeat or just plain beautiful. And all the way up to the very end of his life, he would drive around and CRANK THE TUNES! And I mean loud ... turn them up and feel them ... I personally prefer to dance while driving. In fact, I enjoy dancing while driving so much that I believe half the town of Tahlequah may have seen me doing just that but guess what, I don't care! It is too fun and awesome to care what other people think and I would rather them catch a dose of enthusiasm by laughing at me then to stay serious and bored at a stoplight!

LAUGH!

It was completely normal to be up one level in the living room of Dad's house and to hear him downstairs cracking up! (Which of course made all of us giggle too.) It was also typical for Dad to call me and say, "Oh MY GOD, you have to HEAR THIS ... are you ready?" Then he would read a piece from a book or an article ... and he would barely be able to read because he was laughing so hard. It was completely normal for him and I to be on the phone laughing so hard we could barely talk!

So this is what you need to do: go seek it out. Go find what makes you laugh on the Internet, in a book, or on an old movie. It doesn't matter what medium. Whatever gets you laughing, find it every day.

So here you go, you want to have days that are awesome right? You want an extraordinary life, right? You do want to live the best life possible, right?

Do these things today and every day thereafter and celebrate your awesome life and the decisions you make at the end of the day. Check them off!

1. Remember over and over again, these words: YES! I create my own reality! YES! I can do anything I really want to do and this is my life, my RESPONSIBILITY! And I am making this world a better place!
2. Pick up the POSTURE Sit, stand and walk tall!
3. Make small, BIG and schedule events in your calendar to do "little" things that you enjoy doing!
4. Crank the tunes!
5. Laugh, Laugh, LAUGH until tears are falling down your face!!

And remember, your life consists of moments and all of these moments are up to you. If you fill them with the five action items above, then be proud of yourself, because you have decided to live with enthusiasm all of the time. Your moments make up hours and those same hours make up days, and those days make up weeks, and weeks make up months, and pretty soon your moments make up your whole life. Now, do this all day today (and tomorrow and the next and the next and the next ...) and tell me, HOW IS YOUR LIFE NOW? Welcome to extraordinary living, my friend!

> *"There will never be another bad day!"*
> —Mark Yarnell

DECISION #6

LEARN

"Growth is IMPERATIVE."
—Mark Yarnell

My dad and I are both very early risers and we both also have a morning routine. When I visited him we would always meet in the kitchen while I made my coffee and he poured his water in a big glass. We would give each other a good morning declaration and head to our respective morning places, knowing that in a couple of hours we would meet again to talk.

This decision to learn is critical to your success in extraordinary living and here is why: you must learn to grow and expand as an individual and the sixth decision of the Yarnell 7 ties right back to the second decision which is Action: you can do anything you really want to do. You must learn in order to live an extraordinary life.

"As long as you are green, you're growing.
As soon as you're ripe, you start to rot."
—Raymond Kroc

This is one of my husband's favorite quotes because it reminds him (and me) that you must be growing. Remaining stagnant is moving backwards. There is always movement in one direction or another; there is no standing still in an ever-changing universe. Therefore, you absolutely must continue to be green … new information and growth is a fundamental decision to extraordinary living. You can't move on without it.

There are two modes of learning for extraordinary living: one is internal and one is external.

INTERNAL LEARNING

This is where we grow as individuals. There is not one single day that should go by without learning about how to grow your own self. This can be in any vein of human studies that you want to choose and is very dependent on where you are right now in life. It may be that you are really interested in spirituality or it may be that you are very interested in high performance living. Or maybe both, which is great too.

If you need to learn to drop your past or to discard your fears, there is information out there to help. If you need to learn more about how to push yourself and become who you are meant to be, there is material for that. Always keep in mind that you are here for a reason. Your talents, your outlooks, your capabilities are meant to be expanded and shared with others. Read, watch and listen to everything you possibly can so that every day you are learning to become a stronger, happier and more exceptional person.

EXTERNAL LEARNING

This is when you learn about the world around you. You choose a topic of interest, pick a book, and learn from it. Dad read on science and he read a lot about social sciences and human beings. Most days he would bound upstairs to give me some new information when our morning sessions were over. He would be absolutely JAZZED about what he learned and would take copious notes. His books looked like crazy town ... tabs sticking out, underlines, highlights and next to it on graph paper, he would have notes for his next creation whether it be a piece of writing or a speech.

"Live as if you were to die tomorrow.
Learn as if you were to live forever."
—Mahatma Gandhi

First, commit to one hour a day, in the morning (or at night if you are a night person) to learn. I would highly recommend that you use the old-fashioned method of learning, which is reading a book. Articles are great and in today's world they are extremely accessible thanks to the internet but here is the deal: if you are reading online when you are making the decision to learn on a daily basis, you are way more likely to get distracted and this is the time when you need to work that brain and develop yourself. It is so easy to read a part of one article and then go down the rabbit hole of switching to another article and then checking your email and then looking at Facebook and then and then and then.

If you would like recommendations on books to read, feel free to check out the "Resources" at TheYarnell7.com

For the purpose of living an extraordinary life, choose to read in a **distraction-free** environment. If you are not into reading physical books and you are a big reader of ebooks, that's awesome but make sure you don't have anything else open in your browser or read on a Kindle or some other e-reader.

According to Clifford Nass, professor of communications at Stanford University and author of *The Man Who Lied to His Laptop* with Corina Yen, "The research is unanimous, which is very rare in social sciences, and it says that people who chronically multitask show an enormous range of deficits. They're basically terrible at all sorts of cognitive tasks. Including multitasking."

It is very, very important to watch the studies on the effects of distraction on the human brain. In fact, if you want to study this one subject and get that information out there to the masses and/or to your children, I highly recommend it. This was one of my dad's greatest concerns with humanity. In fact, he refused to even carry a cell phone. If we are constantly looking at our phones, at our computers, and at the TV, and switching between them, how in the world are we really going to get anything done? Learning and creating and action take focus. So commit to one hour a day of focused learning and watch your life soar!

Also, during this time, keep a journal or notebook or something right next to you so that you can take notes about what you are learning, for two reasons. When you read something and then write it down you are learning it way more effectively. Secondly, this is a time when your brain is going to get really creative. When you learn you are also opening up to create.

So when you set yourself up in a routine to learn, keep in mind that ideas will be generated and you must capture those ideas in writing so you don't forget them later. Just imagine your books as wells that spring ideas like no other medium! This is when you grow and reflect and generate magnificent ideas to grow yourself and grow your life and grow the world ... it is critical that you adopt this time to LEARN so do not skip this decision! It sounds simple and sometimes we have a tendency to say, "Yeah, yeah, I got that," but listen, unless you are doing this every single day, you don't got that! So pick a time, pick some books, and give this precious gift to yourself: learn and grow ... the world needs you!

"To be always intending to make a new and better life but never to find time to set about it, is as to put off eating and drinking and sleeping from one day to the next until you're dead."
—Og Mandino

Okay so now that you have made the decision to take at least one hour of undistracted time per day to learn internally and externally, I want to add something else to the mix that will increase your learning time and give you great joy! I recommend that you work on learning and growth with some sort of class that is recorded on a CD or an audiobook that you can download to any of your music mediums and here is why:

According to a study done by the Harvard Health Watch, an average American spends 101 minutes per day driving. Now let's add this up: that means the average person spends almost 12 hours per week in the car. That gives you an extra 48 hours per month to learn! Can you even imagine what you can do with an extra 614 hours per year of learning? The sky's the limit, my friend!

So choose something like *The Yarnell 7* on audio or Tony Robbins or Brendon Burchard or one of the other awesome inspirational people out there and make it a habit to listen as you drive! But remember, every now and then, crank the tunes to keep your enthusiasm at a high level … ya gotta give yourself a dance break sometimes!

Now, look at your new life (it's pretty cool), every single morning (or night if you are one of those owls) you are growing, expanding, creating and living an extraordinary life! Congrats! The world needs you and YOU are there for it!

What do you want to learn?

List three books (or audiobooks or programs) that will teach you how to grow as an individual:

1.

2.

3.

List three books (or audiobooks or programs) that will teach you about a subject that interests you:

1.

2.

3.

Order one or find one in each section and start today! YAY!

DECISION #7

LEADERSHIP

*"A leader is someone who consistently
demonstrates what is possible."*
—Mark Yarnell

"Be the BEST version of yourself that you can be."
—Mark Yarnell

When you make this final decision to be a leader, you are committing to being an example that it is indeed possible to live an extraordinary life! This is a biggie so read on because there are ways you will become a leader that I guarantee, you have never considered.

In the last year of his life, Dad and I were again talking philosophy at his house and I asked him, "So what do you think about your life, Dad?" The questions we posed to each other were fairly large questions; our conversations were not geared toward small talk, ever. He said, "Ya know honey, I have been the best version of Mark Yarnell that I can be." And, I knew then, that he was satisfied with all he did.

The beauty of this statement is twofold: on the one hand, it is very empowering: being the very best human being that we can possible be is certainly what we should all strive for in life. And then this statement is also considerate of being a human and making mistakes.

Sometimes when we think of being a leader, we let that decision slip by and there are generally two reasons: either we think we have made just a few too many mistakes to really BE a leader or we slough off the whole leadership concept because we think leaders are simply bigger than what we can be … both points are worth considering.

Let's start with human error. We all make errors … we make the wrong decisions and say the wrong things but making human errors does not keep us from being great leaders. What does keep us from being great leaders is not learning from and correcting our mistakes. This is when you take the best version of yourself very seriously. The best version makes allowances for mistakes but it does not excuse the repeated decision to make the same mistakes forever. You must learn from your not-so-awesome decisions, take accountability for them, refuse to beat yourself up for them (remember the past is gone) and then move on as a new and improved version of yourself.

So whatever it is that is holding you back from being a leader in the realm of your past, say this statement:

"I made an error when I _____. I take full responsibility for my choice to make this error. However, upon reflection of this error, I release it and I am now new and improved and I will show up to life as the next best version of myself."

If there are multiple behaviors and decisions in your past that you aren't a big fan of, then write everything down in your TY7 journal and simply let them go, either by crossing them out, ripping them up or throwing them away. Similar to being a victim of other people's past behaviors, you need not be a victim of your own. In fact, your errors in life or the negative things that happened in your past are **gold** because this is what people need to hear!

Remember when we talked about your life being your responsibility and we discussed the gifts that come from your past in the form of tragedy or awful experiences? People need to hear from you. They need to know how you have transformed into this extraordinary person, what you have learned and how they too can rise above the past. You are a gift due to your unique past and the way that you can communicate your removal from that past!

> *"I will love the light for it shows me the way, yet I will*
> *endure the darkness because it shows me the stars."*
> —Og Mandino

My dad was very clear about his biggest error (or misstep) in life: for many years he chose to live in addiction. He was extremely forthright about this. When he was considerably younger, he drank alcohol and he drank bigtime … because everything he did was BIGTIME! He knew that this wasn't exactly a good or productive way to live and many, many years ago, he put a stop to it.

(A note to all addicts: I realize that addiction is a disease but the reason I can attribute my Dad's decision to stop drinking as an option is because as addicts, we all have the power to make the NO decision every single day. Obviously, if we couldn't, AA would not exist!)

But, imagine if he thought, "Ya know what, I really can't be a leader because I am/was an alcoholic so it would be extremely hypocritical of me to go out and be a leader." Countless lives would not be the same and as a result, the world would be a different place based on that one decision. Instead he kicked it, acknowledged his mistake, and moved on. You can take the largest errors and turn them around and move on. It is absolutely ridiculous to not share who you are in the world just because you made some mistakes, even big ones!

Now, acknowledge your errors, acknowledge that you are making different decisions and you are now being the best version of yourself that you can be and **move on down the road**!

BEING A LEADER BY EXAMPLE

The next part about being a leader that tends to be prohibitive is that we think, "I am no Martin Luther King Jr. My life is really not that large. I am just a regular bloke and even if I make my life incredible, I am still a regular bloke. No, no Martin here. Thanks for playing'."

Listen closely: Every single interaction with another human being gives you an opportunity to help the other person live a better life. This is not an exaggeration. I once finished reading a book with one very, very long-lasting clear image in my head. The author was feeling like he wasn't having an impact on the world and then he closed his eyes and in his mind's eye he saw a stadium and the stadium was filled with people and the stadium of people were standing up clapping for him and he then knew that thousands upon thousands of people had been positively affected by him.

Now, as that author was feeling, you might similarly say to me: "But Amy, my goals are not to be a public speaker and an author that changes the world!" And my response is: NO NEED! Your very existence is impacting the world!

Here is one possible scenario and an example dialogue that may sound incredibly simplistic but I want you to understand how important this really is ...

You are at the grocery store shopping and you are happy but a bit fatigued because you have had a long and productive day. You approach the register and as the register attendant starts bagging your groceries, he asks,

"How are you this evening?"

Now this is when you will see people make the biggest error they can possibly make when dealing with other human beings and that is simply that they aren't paying attention. Checking out in a store is so familiar to 99.9 percent of people in developed nations that 99.8 percent of people don't consider it an opportunity for leadership.

But leadership comes in many forms, from the most mundane to the Martin Luther King Jr. level and all are equally important. When you are actually interacting with another human being, realize it, put the phone down, quit thinking about your life and note: there is another human being here.

Look straight at the other person and pay attention. (This is another human being after all.)

YOU: "I am GREAT … how about you? Are you having a nice day?"

Now, listen. Generally, the person on the other end will offer some kind of complaint in response. Isn't that weird? Human beings have a tendency to complain but LEADERS do not. Listen kindly, care about what they are saying (again, this *is* another human being) and be there for them. This is the time when you can offer encouragement or general happiness to the other person—remember you NURTURE others. Oftentimes, you also need to practice your E decision and show a little excitement. Either way, talk with them … engage!

The clerk has finished ringing you up, you give him the money, he gives you the receipt and says "Have a nice evening."

YOU: "I hope you have a FANTASTIC evening too! Thank you so much and it was nice talking with you!"

Choose your own approach but remember your "E." Be EXCITED about life because you *are* excited about life and your enthusiasm will catch. And do you know what happens? It creates a ripple effect.

Because you demonstrated your enthusiasm and your capacity to care with the grocery clerk, he will be uplifted by a degree and do you know what he will do with that? He will give it to the next person in line. And then by the end of his shift, all of the sudden, the grocer is having a great time at work, having a few laughs and he has no idea why and it doesn't matter. And then this keeps going: his coworkers are uplifted and the people checking out with the happy grocery attendant are uplifted and then those people go home and their entire family is uplifted and this goes on and on and on and on.

Set the bar for others! Lead by example!

Now take a moment to imagine what this world would be like if we all talked to each other with care and enthusiasm, and if we all decided that every stranger we encountered was awesome and deserving of a smile and a conversation! I am irrevocably convinced that these actions which seem tiny are actually huge. Picture the stadium of people up clapping for you for no one specific reason. Those are all of the people you affected. You absolutely must be a TY7 example, which, by default, is being a leader!

The week after Dad died, our family was doing the ugly job of making sure everyone who knew him also knew that he had departed. And as we planned the funeral and made our lists of people to talk to, we also realized that someone had to visit "Dad's stores." True story: someone had to take on the task of visiting the convenient stores, the dry cleaners, the boat store, the tire store ... someone had to go tell all of these people that Dad had passed away because over the years of making people's lives better in the stores, he had built relationships with all of them. And these people were strangers to us, but Dad saw them on a regular basis and they *loved* him. Now this, my friend, is LEADERSHIP: the love and care you give to complete and total strangers is a big deal. You don't have to be a Martin. You can just create the endless ripple of simple care and enthusiasm and change the world!

Who did you demonstrate leadership to today?

Think through your day and make a list the "strangers" you encountered. After each person, explain how you demonstrated TY7 Leadership.

1.

2.

3.

4.

5.

THE CHILDREN ARE WATCHING YOU!

"Kids don't remember what you try to teach them.
They remember what you are."
—Jim Henson

It's Not Easy Being Green: And Other Things to Consider

It is so easy to forget that you are a leader in your own household. But your ability to change the lives of your young ones is incredible. They are looking to you and modeling your behavior. This responsibility is enormous because you are planting the seeds for their lives. Obviously, even with my dad's shortcomings (we all have them), what he taught me and what he became in life, enabled me to sit here and type these words. And even if only one person hears me and integrates these decisions into his life, the world will be forever changed.

When considering yourself as a leader of your children, your tendency will be to think about the big actions you take as a parent: the important conversations and big accomplishments, but take the time to consider the seemingly small actions. For instance, when you and your children are in the car, would you rather them watch you having a temper tantrum about the traffic or do you want them to learn how to do a dance off? Would you rather them watch a phone or a dvd or would you rather them hear your audiobook playing about how to live an extraordinary life? Would you rather them see you ignore the grocery attendant or see you respect and enjoy the people around you? When you look at the small moments, you will begin to see that your simple ways of being are in fact the fundamental building blocks for how your children will choose to live their lives.

If you were looking at my life from the outside, I am sure you would guess that my favorite memories of my Dad are during our trips to the Caribbean or Mexico or Europe or any of our other wild adventures. But you would be incorrect. My favorite two memories of my dad are before he became the legendary best-selling author/speaker/network marketer. One is of Dad and I playing Donkey Kong at the 7-Eleven in Austin, Texas. The other is of my dad sitting across from me at a seated Pac Man machine in the lobby of a hotel while he loudly tapped his hands to the beat of the Pac Man song as I was eating a blueberry muffin and giggling madly. It didn't matter where we were; what mattered is that we were laughing and playing and having a blast together! He instilled enjoyment of life into my framework from the very beginning.

Please remember at all times that you are demonstrating what is possible for your friends, your significant other, your family and especially your children. If you can be a leader by example for the youth of today, your kids or others, you are doing a great service for not only them, but for humanity.

How did you demonstrate true leadership today to children or young adults? Do not reflect on what you did per se, but rather reflect on who you are and who you were being around them. Were you enthusiastic? Did they see you learning? Did they see you work on your Actions and Goals? Did they see you nurture others?

I demonstrated TY7 Leadership to children when I:

IF YOU WANT TO BE A MARTIN ... If you do not wish to be a Martin, great! However, it is imperative that you know that you can be a Martin. Let's review. These are the decisions you have made:

YES! I create my own reality!

ACTION! I can do anything, I really want to do!

RESPONSIBILITY! My Life is my responsibility!

NURTURE! I nurture other human beings and I have goals bigger than myself!

ENTHUSIASM! I am shining my light!

LEARN! My growth is imperative!

LEADERSHIP! I am the best version of myself that I can be and I demonstrate what is possible.

If you want to be a Martin, explain what you want to do, why you want to do it, and how you are going to do it right here. Remember to add this section to your Goals/Actions and Time Map section as well!

Take a moment to really consider what this world would be like if everyone adopted these seven decisions into their lives. Even if they understood the first two decisions, our world would shift. If everyone walked around and knew that they were creating their own reality and that they could do anything they really wanted to do, all of life would shift. Can you imagine?

Now if you make each one of these decisions and live by *The Yarnell 7*, and you want to be a Martin Luther King Jr.? Well, all the power to you! Go do it! **There are no limitations on your**

present or your future. Zero. So if you want to change the world from a true stadium-standing-ovation position, then you just go for it. There are plenty of resources at www.TheYarnell7.com for you to use. If you want to speak, speak. If you want to write, then write. If you want to sing, sing. GO ON … push it!

You have a responsibility to all of the world and every single person counts. Recognize that your decision to live an extraordinary life has now changed the planet **forever**. *At any given moment, you are either a leader by choice or a leader by example. Both count.*

Remember, friend and TY7 Leader: everything is within your grasp. There are **no limitations.** Now go demonstrate what is possible!

And as Mark Yarnell would say:

"I will see you on the beaches of the world!"

✔ #1 **Y**es
(I create my own reality!)

✔ #2 **A**ction
(I can do anything that I realy want to do!)

✔ #3 **R**esponsibility
(My life is my responsibility!)

✔ #4 **N**urture
(I nurture others and I have goals bigger than myself!)

✔ #5 **E**nthusiasm
(I am shining my light!)

✔ #6 **L**earn
(My growth is imperative!)

✔ #7 **L**eadership
(I am the best version of myself that I can be and I demonstrate what is possible!)

About Mark B. Yarnell

Over a twenty-nine-year career in Network Marketing, Mark Yarnell became a legend in the industry and earned a reputation as one of the most passionate and respected advocates of the profession. He was irrevocably convinced that Network Marketing is a force for good in the world, an equalizer, and the last bastion of free enterprise.

Mark grew up in Springfield, Missouri. His high school debating skills earned him a full scholarship to Drury College. During his four years of college, Mark won the national extemporaneous speaking competition two times and was awarded the "Best Debater" distinction at thirty-one collegiate debate tournaments.

In 1979, he attended seminary and studied stress management at the Menninger Foundation in Topeka, Kansas. He served as a stress management consultant for the Hills Medical/Sports Complex and published a recording called "Relaxation, Imagery and Cancer."

Mark was an accomplished author, orator, and international business leader. In 1986, he joined an upstart network marketing company and ultimately developed an international organization of more than 300,000 marketing representatives in twenty-one countries.

Mark ultimately touched the lives of millions. He believed that there is a seed of greatness in everyone. One of his greatest joys was mentoring others to reach their full potential. He influenced others through his example, eleven published books, incredible speeches, countless articles, blog posts, videos and recordings.

His bestselling book *Your First Year in Network Marketing* is considered a veritable bible of the profession.

Mark was the first and only person from network marketing to serve as Contributing Editor to *SUCCESS* Magazine. He and Dr. Charles King of Harvard University co-created the first certification course in Network Marketing taught at the University of Illinois, Chicago from 1993-2011.

Mark was honored and recognized internationally with numerous awards including the American Dream Award. He was named the Greatest Networker in the World by *Upline* Magazine and indoctrinated into the Network Marketing Hall of Fame.

As a noted philanthropist, Mark supported a variety of charitable organizations. He founded The Eagles, a literacy organization for penitentiary inmates and the School of Sobriety, the only free treatment program in Nevada for alcoholics and addicts at the time. His charitable work earned him the Nevada Philanthropist of the Year Award from the Washington Times.

In his last fourteen years, Mark and his wife Valerie, resided in the beautiful mountains of British Columbia, Canada, where they lived a dream life while pursuing their passion for building a network marketing organization together.

Mark read voraciously and wrote daily. He was particularly passionate about the family, Valerie and her two children, Christine and Eric Perkio, and his daughter, Amy Yarnell. He mesmerized the grandchildren with his music, magic tricks and playful nature. Mark valued close friends, fellow networkers, philosophical debates, paragliding, gold panning, fly-fishing, and fly-tying. He was passionate about playing a variety of musical instruments and treasured communing with nature.

Mark was truly inspiring: "I've lived a Zip-a-Dee-Doo-Dah life," he said. "I've squeezed every ounce of joy out of every single day. It's been an absolute blast!" And he encouraged each of us to become the best possible version of ourselves while living a life of freedom.

A Special Thank You to TY7 Decision Makers:

I am so excited for you! This is your first day of living with ALL 7 decisions! It is imperative that you stay with these decisions ... so please take your book everywhere you go and continue using your worksheets. Be a TY7 Decision Maker every single day and every single moment of the rest of your life and watch everything change!

If you need more worksheets, go to "Worksheets" at www.TheYarnell7.com and download them for free!

If you want to see what resources that I find extraordinary, go to "Resources" at www.TheYarnell7.com.

A HUGE thank you to all of the TY7 Decision Makers who have finished this book and who have also left a review on Amazon! We have a much greater shot at making this world a better place if more people find out about *The Yarnell 7*. The more reviews, the greater the chances! Can you even imagine what our world would look like if everyone decided to live an extraordinary life?

This is a time for celebration, so let's do it! Go to the "Winners" www.TheYarnell7.com and enter to win numerous, awesome prizes! You could win anything from an autographed copy of *The Yarnell 7* to a Kindle or a TY7 Coaching Call!

With extraordinary gratitude,

THE YARNELL 7 DECISION MAKER
WORKSHEETS

Most people have "To Do" lists but TY7 Decision Makers have a "TY7 List" list. I recommend that you go to "Worksheets" at www.TheYarnell7.com print these sheets out and start a TY7 Binder. But feel free to use these until you use them up!

TY7 LIST

Every single day, you should fill out the line next to each of your TY7 Decisions:

YES! I create my own reality! Today I

_____

ACTION! I can do anything I really want to do! Today I

_____

RESPONSIBILITY! Today I

_____

NURTURE! Today I

_____

ENTHUSIASM! Today I

_____

LEARN! Today I learned

_____

LEADERSHIP! Today I

_____

This world needs TY7 Decision Makers! So make this list every day and celebrate your victories every night! CONGRATULATIONS!

DECISION #1: YES! Daily Catch & Change Sheet

If you catch yourself with a negative THOUGHT, change it immediately and write it below. Then put a big X over it and write down your NEW thought.

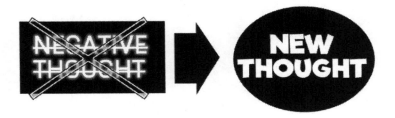

If you catch yourself with a negative REACTION, write it here and then put a big X over it and write down your NEW reaction.

If you catch yourself with a negative FEELING, write it here
and then put a big X over it and write down your NEW feeling.

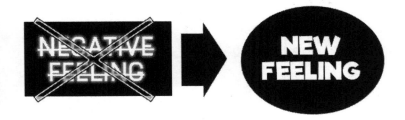

DECISION #2 ACTION!

Pretend like you are a kid in a candy store once again. Look all around this beautiful world we live in and pick what you really want to do while you are here on Planet Earth! List those awesome choices right here:

FREE YOURSELF OF FEAR

What is your number one fear?

Commit to doing it anyway. What is the first step to combatting this fear?

Step One: What is the soonest date and time you can take the first step to overcoming this False Evidence Appearing Real? Make a decision right now.

Additional Steps:

Take these additional steps and schedule them.

Step Two:

Scheduled Date:

Step Three:

Scheduled Date

TIME SECTION:

"I was kidding myself when I said I had no time! I said that about the following extraordinary goals, but I realize now that how I manage my time is my decision."

Where are you spending your time? Make block segments below from the hour you get up to the hour you go to sleep:

My Monday morning hours are from _____ to _____ and this is what I do:

My Tuesday morning hours are from _____ to _____ and this is what I do:

My Wednesday morning hours are from _____ to _____ and this is what I do:

My Thursday morning hours are from _____ to _____ and this is what I do:

My Friday morning hours are from _____ to _____ and this is what I do:

My Saturday morning hours are from _____ to _____ and this is what I do:

My Sunday morning hours are from _____ to _____ and this is what I do:

My Monday DAY hours are from _____ to _____ and this is what I do:

My Tuesday DAY hours are from _____ to _____ and this is what I do:

My Wednesday DAY hours are from _____ to _____ and this is what I do:

My Thursday DAY hours are from _____ to _____ and this is what I do:

My Friday DAY hours are from _____ to _____ and this is what I do:

My Saturday DAY hours are from _____ to _____ and this is what I do:

My Sunday DAY hours are from _____ to _____ and this is what I do:

My Monday EVE & NIGHTTIME hours are from _____ to _____ and this is what I do:

My Tuesday EVE & NIGHTTIME hours are from _____ to _____ and this is what I do:

My Wednesday EVE & NIGHTTIME hours are from _____ to _____ and this is what I do:

My Thursday EVE & NIGHTTIME hours are from _____ to _____ and this is what I do:

My Friday EVE & NIGHTTIME hours are from _____ to _____ and this is what I do:

My Saturday EVE & NIGHTTIME hours are from
_____ to _____ and this is what I do:

My Sunday EVE & NIGHTTIME hours are from _____
to _____ and this is what I do:

Now, look at your candy store list above and write down four goals that you will accomplish in the next 12 months. Then write down your Top Three actions for each goal.

MY FOUR EXTRAORDINARY GOALS THIS YEAR ARE:

GOAL #1:

Action 1:

Action 2:

Action 3:

GOAL #2:

Action 1:

Action 2:

Action 3:

GOAL #3:

Action 1:

Action 2:

Action 3:

GOAL #4:

Action 1:

Action 2:

Action 3:

Now look back at the previous Time Map and mark out the time blocks that are senseless and re-write your new Time Map with your first three actions toward your four goals below. Every single day, review this Time Map/ Goal/Action section and keep adjusting it accordingly by adding your new sets of Actions toward the completion of your goals. (When this one gets overused, download new free ones in the Worksheets section at www.TheYarnell7.com.) DO NOT DELAY. Make the decision to start RIGHT NOW. Go live an extraordinary life already!

NEW TIME MAP with ACTIONS toward GOALS:

My Monday morning hours are from _____ to _____.

This is what I will do during those hours (Break the hours to smaller chunks):

From _____ to _____, I will:

From _____ to _____, I will:

From _____ to _____, I will:

My Tuesday Monday morning hours are from _____ to _____.

This is what I will do during those hours (Break the hours to smaller chunks):

From _____ to _____, I will:

From _____ to _____, I will:

From _____ to _____, I will:

My Wednesday morning hours are from _____ to _____.

This is what I will do during those hours (Break the hours to smaller chunks):

From _____ to _____, I will:

From _____ to _____, I will:

From _____ to _____, I will:

My Thursday morning hours are from _____ to _____.

This is what I will do during those hours (Break the hours to smaller chunks):

From _____ to _____, I will:

From _____ to _____, I will:

From _____ to _____, I will:

My Friday morning hours are from _____ to _____.

This is what I will do during those hours (Break the hours to smaller chunks):

From _____ to _____, I will:

From _____ to _____, I will:

From _____ to _____, I will:

My Saturday morning hours are from _____ to _____.

This is what I will do during those hours (Break the hours to smaller chunks):

From _____ to _____, I will:

From _____ to _____, I will:

From _____ to _____, I will:

My Sunday morning hours are from _____ to _____.

This is what I will do during those hours (Break the hours to smaller chunks):

From _____ to _____, I will:

From _____ to _____, I will:

From _____ to _____, I will:

My Monday DAY hours are from _____ to _____.

From _____ to _____, I will:

From _____ to _____, I will:

From _____ to _____, I will:

My Tuesday DAY hours are from _____ to _____.

From _____ to _____, I will:

From _____ to _____, I will:

From _____ to _____, I will:

My Wednesday DAY hours are from _____ to _____.

From _____ to _____, I will:

From _____ to _____, I will:

From _____ to _____, I will:

My Thursday DAY hours are from _____to _____.

From _____ to _____, I will:

From _____ to _____, I will:

From _____ to _____, I will:

My Friday DAY hours are from _____to _____.

From _____ to _____, I will:

From _____ to _____, I will:

From _____ to _____, I will:

My Saturday DAY hours are from _____to _____.

From _____ to _____, I will:

From _____ to _____, I will:

From _____ to _____, I will:

My Sunday DAY hours are from _____ to _____.

From _____ to _____, I will:

From _____ to _____, I will:

From _____ to _____, I will:

My Monday EVE & NIGHT-TIME hours are from _____ to
_____.

From _____ to _____, I will:

From _____ to _____, I will:

From _____ to _____, I will:

My Tuesday EVE & NIGHT-TIME hours are from _____ to
_____.

From _____ to _____, I will:

From _____ to _____, I will:

From _____ to _____, I will:

My Wednesday EVE & NIGHT-TIME hours are from _____
to _____.

From _____ to _____, I will:

From _____ to _____, I will:

From _____ to _____, I will:

My Thursday EVE & NIGHT-TIME hours are from _____ to _____.

From _____ to _____, I will:

From _____ to _____, I will:

From _____ to _____, I will:

My Friday EVE & NIGHT-TIME hours are from _____ to _____.

From _____ to _____, I will:

From _____ to _____, I will:

From _____ to _____, I will:

My Saturday EVE & NIGHT-TIME hours are from _____ to
_____.

From _____ to _____, I will:

From _____ to _____, I will:

From _____ to _____, I will:

My Sunday EVE & NIGHT-TIME hours are from _____ to
_____.

From _____ to _____, I will:

From _____ to _____, I will:

From _____ to _____, I will:

DECISION #3 RESPONSIBILITY

My Life, My Responsibility!

THE PAST IS GONE!

Take this moment and write down two things in your past that you tend to point at as a reason for your lack of extraordinary behavior.

POINTS IN THE PAST:

1.

2.

Now: cross them out. I want you to put a big, bad X over each one right now. :Next: take a loose piece of paper and write down something that happened in your past that you point to as an excuse for your lack of extraordinary living, now rip it up into tiny little pieces and throw it in the trash can! This is your life, not your mom's, not your dad's, not your Aunt Tilly's so throw the past away!

I am in charge of me! Catch & Change!

Any time you think or utter the words:

"She (or he) made me _____ (insert the negative feeling here)," Catch yourself and change it!

State the following: No one can make ME feel anything. I choose to feel the way I feel. My decision.

Did you catch yourself giving the power of your own emotions and your own feelings away to anyone else? If so, list them here and then write a bit about how you changed your perspective.

REACTIVE THOUGHT: At first I thought I was feeling that way because:

RESOLUTION: And then I realized that I was feeling that way because:

DECISION #4 NURTURE

I nurture others consistently!

Who did you listen to today? How did you contribute to their lives? Do this for seven days and then keep on going in your worksheets.

Day One:

Day Two:

Day Three:

Day Four:

Day Five:

Day Six:

Day Seven:

What concerns you most about our world?

What can you contribute? How can you make this world a better place? Is there an organization you would like to contribute to with time or with money? Or is there an organization you would like to create?

DECISION #5 ENTHUSIASM!

From Molehills to Mountains!

What are some small activities that you really enjoy?

Now schedule them in your actual calendar and be excited because life is FUN! Look at your scheduled activities every day and look forward to them!

Did you crank up the tunes today? (Consider dancing like a wild person … don't worry, you can do this safely in your car and so far no one has sent me to an institution. [wink] I think you're safe to dance in your seat … and it is SO worth it!)

Make a list of all of the things that you can read or watch or do that make you laugh out loud. Schedule them if you have to, but just make sure you incorporate a good belly laugh into your life on a daily basis.

DECISION #6 LEARN

What do you want to learn?

List three books (or audiobooks or programs) that will teach you how to grow as an individual:

1.

2.

3.

List three books (or audiobooks or programs) that will teach you about a subject that interests you:

1.

2.

3.

Order one or find one in each section and start today! YAY! So excited for you! Incorporate this learning time into your TIME MAP!

DECISION #7 LEADERSHIP

Who did you demonstrate leadership to today?

Think through your day and make a list the "strangers" you encountered. After each person, explain how you demonstrated TY7 Leadership.

1.

2.

3.

4.

5.

IF YOU WANT TO BE A MARTIN ... If you do not wish to be a Martin, great! However, it is imperative that you know that you can be a Martin. Let's review. These are the decisions you have made:

YES! I create my own reality!

ACTION! I can do anything, I really want to do!

RESPONSIBILITY! My Life is my responsibility!

NURTURE! I nurture other human beings and I have goals bigger than myself!

ENTHUSIASM! I am shining my light!

LEARN! My growth is imperative!

LEADERSHIP! I am the best version of myself that I can be and I demonstrate what is possible.

If you want to be a Martin, explain what you want to do, why you want to do it, and how you are going to do it right here. Remember to add this section to your Goals/Actions and Time Map section as well!

Keep this handy so that you continue to make the core decisions that will ensure you live an extraordinary life! Check them off every single day!

✔ #1 **Y**es
(I create my own reality!)

✔ #2 **A**ction
(I can do anything that I realy want to do!)

✔ #3 **R**esponsibility
(My life is my responsibility!)

✔ #4 **N**urture
(I nurture others and I have goals bigger than myself!)

✔ #5 **E**nthusiasm
(I am shining my light!)

✔ #6 **L**earn
(My growth is imperative!)

✔ #7 **L**eadership
(I am the best version of myself that I can be and I demonstrate what is possible!)

Acknowledgments

As far as friends and family are concerned, I am convinced that I am the most fortunate woman in the world. I hope that I show you how much you mean to me and my creative life. First and foremost, thank you Mom for providing me with a nurturing and grounded environment; you have shown me balance and unconditional love and I would never be who I am today without your loving support. Thank you to my husband, Kelon, for your steady comfort, support, and love. Thank you, Mum, for loving Dad and me as your own and for giving him a beautiful home and perfect love. Thank you, Nick, for always loving me as your own. Thank you, Christine, for loving my Dad and me as your own and for creating and sharing Kennedy and Charlotte with us and the world. Thank you, Eric, for all of the laughter, love, and warmth that you bring to every adventure. Thank you, Grandpa, for showing me how to be dependable and kind. Thank you, Ham, for all of your love. Thank you, Drew Haley, for being such a wonderful friend, videographer, and graphic artist. Thank you, Edna Kimble, for being a truly amazing friend and mentor. Thank you, Julie DeLong, for being my very best friend since childhood and for your undying love and support as a fellow writer and creator. Thank you, Heather Mulhern, for being a lovely light in my life. Thank you, Dylan Russell, for taking on the illustrations; you are incredibly talented. Thank you to my awesome editor, Spencer Borup; your encouraging, uplifting attitude and knowledge have been just what I needed to move forward. Thank you to my coach, Ramy Vance, for your unwavering enthusiasm and steady stream of knowledge and thank you to Chandler Bolt for going for it and creating SPS. Thank you, Mandy Stapleford, for being the absolute best accountability partner that I could ever wish for;

this process would not have been nearly as amazing without you in it. Thank you to all of Dad's friends who have encouraged and loved me through this process. And of course, thank you Daddy Beeka; without you, this work would not exist and nor would I. I love you.

Notes

Made in the USA
San Bernardino, CA
July 2018